KEEPING US ENGAGED

KEEPING US ENGAGED

Student Perspectives (and Research-Based Strategies)
on What Works and Why

Christine Harrington and
50 College Students

Foreword by José Antonio Bowen

1996–2021 25TH ANNIVERSARY

Sty/us
PUBLISHING, LLC.

STERLING, VIRGINIA

Sty/us

COPYRIGHT © 2021 BY STYLUS PUBLISHING, LLC

Published by Stylus Publishing, LLC
22883 Quicksilver Drive
Sterling, Virginia 20166-2019

Library of Congress Cataloging-in-Publication Data
Names: Harrington, Christine, 1971- author.
Title: Keeping us engaged : student perspectives (and research-based strategies) on what works and why / Christine Marie Harrington and 50 college students ; foreword by José Antonio Bowen.
Description: Sterling, Virginia : Stylus Publishing, LLC, 2021. | Includes bibliographical references and index. |
Identifiers: LCCN 2021004379 | ISBN 9781642670813 (paperback) | ISBN 9781642670806 (hardcover) | ISBN 9781642670837 (ebook) | ISBN 9781642670820 (adobe pdf)
Subjects: LCSH: College teaching. | Motivation in education. | Academic achievement--Psychological aspects.
Classification: LCC LB2331 .H3177 2021 | DDC 378.1/25--dc23
LC record available at https://lccn.loc.gov/2021004379

13-digit ISBN: 978-1-64267-080-6 (cloth)
13-digit ISBN: 978-1-64267-081-3 (paperback)
13-digit ISBN: 978-1-64267-082-0 (library networkable e-edition)
13-digit ISBN: 978-1-64267-083-7 (consumer e-edition)

Printed in the United States of America

All first editions printed on acid-free paper
that meets the American National Standards Institute
Z39-48 Standard.

Bulk Purchases

Quantity discounts are available for use in workshops and for staff development.

Call 1-800-232-0223

First Edition, 2021

*To all my students and the student contributors
of this book*

CONTENTS

FOREWORD   xi
José Antonio Bowen

ACKNOWLEDGMENTS   xiii
Thank You to the Student Contributors   xiv

INTRODUCTION   1
Overview of This Book   4
Overview of Student Contributors   6

1   STARTING POSITIVE: THE FIRST DAY OF CLASS AND
THE SYLLABUS   9
Engaging Students on the First Day of Class   9
Creating a Sense of Belonging   10
     Learning Student Names and Interests   10
         Getting to Know Me, Rosalyn Stoa   11
     Icebreakers   12
         Creative Icebreakers, Tyler Goslin   14
         Large Class Introductions, Alison Larsen   15
         An Online Icebreaker, Robert J. Portella (online class)   16
         Online Icebreaker in a Cohort Program, Amy Hankins (online class)   17
Generating Excitement   18
     Sharing Your Enthusiasm and Passion, Eric Imlach   19
     Engaging Student Survey, Aditya Shah   20
     Explaining the Why Behind Textbook Selections, Kristi Gundhus   22
Developing Knowledge and Skills   23
     Previewing Final Exam Questions and Using Social Media,
     Samantha Alger-Feser   23
     Getting Students Excited About a Semester-Long Project,
     Amanda Galazzo   25
     Solving Complicated Math Problems on Day One, Cayleigh Keenan   26
Using the Syllabus as an Engagement Tool   27
     Transparent, Clear Expectations in the Syllabus, Michael Daidone   28
     Hidden Bonus, Madison Hilton   29
     Choosing Assignments, Caleb E. Morris   30
     Student Choice, Michaela White   32
Faculty Reflection Questions   33

2   POWER OF RELATIONSHIPS   35
    Connecting With Students During Class   36
        Getting-to-Know-You Pecha Kucha, Shadiquah Hordge   37
        Using Writing to Foster Relationships, Vidish Parikh   38
        Tapping Into Student Interests, Michael Daidone   39
    Interacting With Students Outside of Class   41
        An Individual Meeting With a Disengaged Student, Joshua Allen Brown   42
        Deeper Levels of Learning, Michaela White   44
        Gaining Confidence and Discovering Interests, Jessica M. Robbins   45
    Assisting Students Struggling With Personal Challenges   46
        Dealing With Family Illness and Loss, Wm. Dean Martin   47
        Mental Health Referral, Amalia Carmencita Rodas   49
    Serving as Career Mentors   50
        Advising Days, Sarah Harvey   50
        Invitation to Work in a Lab, David Lont   51
        Changing Career Paths, Serena Rose Arandia   53
    Helping Students Build a Professional Network   53
        Interviewing Industry Professionals, Jaclyn Bonacorda   54
        Networking Connections, Rosalyn Stoa   55
        Creating a Professional Network Among Advisees, Danielle V. Lewis   56
    Faculty Reflection Questions   57

3   TEACHING STRATEGIES   59
    Making It Personal   60
        Sharing Personal Experiences, Joshua Allen Brown   61
        A Tailored Learning Experience, Laura Goldfarb   62
        A Note Card Activity, Benjamin Sackler   64
        Discovering Your Passion, Genevieve Jaser   65
    Using Demonstrations   66
        Interactive Demonstration in Physics, David Lont   67
        Examples and Demonstrations, Samantha Alger-Feser   68
        Videos and Synchronous Meetings in an Online Course, Amy Hankins
        (online class)   69
    Using Collaborative Activities   70
        Discussions   71
            Student-Driven Discussions, Kayla Jasper   71
            Using Thought Organizers in Discussions, Claire Maloney   73
            Online Discussions, Sarah Lyman Kravits (online class)   74
        Group Projects   75
            Semester-Long Group Work, Sara Idol   75
            Peer-Supported Learning, Turner Smith   76
            Online Group Project, Edwin S. Lee (online class)   78
            A Community-Based Learning Experience, Rosemary Brockett   80
    Faculty Reflection Questions   81

4   MEANINGFUL ASSIGNMENTS   83
    Building Foundational Knowledge   83
        Prelecture Quizzes, Vidish Parikh   84
        Writing to Learn, Elena St. Amour   85

Using Authentic Assignments to Promote Learning 86
    Marketing Simulation, Joseph Bonacorda 87
    Creating Sexual Education Curricula, Kaitlynn Ely 89
    Developing a Proposal, Carrie Hachadurian 90
    Planning a Career Fair, Jaclyn Bonacorda 92
Pushing Students Outside Their Comfort Zone 93
    Speaking Up in Class, Kayla Wathen 93
    New Forms of Writing, Brett Hurst 94
    Cultural Interview and Research Project, Cayleigh Keenan 96
    Experiencing a Different Religion, Benjamin Sackler 97
Fostering Creativity 98
    Creative Essay Portfolio, Julie Bechtel Patino 98
    Creativity in Assignments, Kristina M. Perrelli 100
    Finding My Voice, Kara Infelise 101
Service-Learning 102
    Service-Learning at an Assisted Living Facility, Davis Wilson 103
    Designing a Sustainable Pub, Rosemary Brockett 104
Faculty Reflection Questions 106

5   FEEDBACK 107
Formative Assessment Opportunities 108
    Project Check-Ins, Jaclyn Bonacorda 110
    Breaking Down a Major Assignment, Kayla Jasper 111
    Numerous Feedback Opportunities, Caleb E. Morris 112
    Ungraded Assignments, Annie Kelly 113
Incorporating Peer Feedback Opportunities 115
    Peer Review Sessions, Elena St. Amour 115
    Layers of Peer Feedback, Robert J. Portella (online class) 116
    Graded Peer Feedback, Sarah Lyman Kravits (online class) 117
Giving Students Opportunities to Revise 119
    Pushing Me to Improve, Kara Infelise 119
    Building Skills Through Revision Opportunities, Amy Hankins
    (online course) 121
    Second Chance, Erin Stern 122
    Required Revisions, Ryan Harrington 123
Providing Feedback to High-Achieving Students 124
    Supporting Me as an "A" Student, Kayla Wathen 125
    Pushing Me to Excel, Michael Daidone 126
    Reinforcing Strengths, Christina Christodoulou 127
Faculty Reflection Questions 129

REFERENCES 131

ABOUT THE AUTHOR 145

INDEX 147

S ometimes the obvious is staring you right in the face.

The last 50 years have seen an explosion of research in educational best practices, cognitive science, design, and the psychology of learning. With the creation of centers for teaching and learning on most campuses, the substantial growth of a literature of pedagogy, and even consideration of the practice and scholarship of teaching and learning in tenure decisions (okay, perhaps still a way to go on that last one), faculty are no longer limited to what they observed about teaching in graduate school.

No more hushed conversations around the copy machine about better assignments. No more throat-cutting gestures from colleagues when we bring up teaching in faculty meetings. No more wide-eyed, "Are you kidding me?" looks from advisers when graduate students ask if there will be any training or instruction in teaching before they are assigned a 500-person intro class. And who can forget that feeling of having finished all 45 handwritten lecture outlines before the semester? You might still be having that teaching naked dream the night before your first class of the semester, but our conversations about teaching are truly unrecognizable for those of us old enough to remember classrooms without computers and video projectors. If you still think of a syllabus as a list of topics you will "cover," or you are keeping your old overhead projector sheets (for the young'uns, imagine clear plastic sheets that fed into a copier and were then placed on wheeled overhead projectors—where you could write on them!), it's a new day.

The new pedagogical literature is full of evidence-based ideas and road-tested best practices. And yet, for all that research and assessment on learning, a student perspective has often been missing. What really engages students? What feels authentic and what feels fake? How are our best intentions interpreted? Especially in 2020, as we have all struggled with less bandwidth, we have seen firsthand the importance of really listening and understanding the student experience.

The students here come from a broad cross-section of American universities: large, small, public, private, liberal arts, technical, elite, and regional. The student backgrounds are also varied: undergraduate, graduate, full time, part time, online, in person, first generation, traditional age, underrepresented, adults, and so forth. This is a well-conceived and highly organized way to hear real stories about what students actually perceive in our class-rooms. Organizing this book around key moments in our interactions with students was an inspired move.

We know that first impressions are important, but in these student stories we get to hear how easily we can create more motivation and belonging on the first day of class. We know, too, that relationships matter, but here is massive and powerful support for the many ways faculty can go deeper in offering both personal and professional support that can have impact. You have no doubt heard that students value "real world" examples, assignments, and connections, but the students in this book make the broader point that this is really about finding meaning and value in what we are asking them to do. Similarly, we already know that feedback is an important part of learning, but it is revealing to hear how much of this is about our belief in their ability to improve.

We know now that engagement, motivation, and trust are prerequisites for learning, and here, at last, is a guide for what really matters to students. Here is the texture, detail, and nuance to the broad picture we have gained from pedagogical research. It is especially useful to hear about the unantici-pated benefits from things we do. Most faculty, for example, can see the value of an icebreaker to share something on the syllabus that interests you (see p. 16, this volume), but I, at least, did not anticipate that students would also find this a good way to acknowledge their fears and feel more connected. If we really want to put students first, these stories are transformative.

Our guide is the sensitive, prolific, and clear-eyed Professor Christine Harrington. Her many books, research, good advice, and deep caring for students precede her. Her work has always been both scholarly and practi-cal, and this is another book full of insight that is immediately applicable. Still, you will be astonished at how many simple things you can do tomor-row. Rarely have I read a book where on almost every page I said (usually in sequence), "Aha," "Now I get it," and finally, "I must do that."

You should probably still put fewer words on your PowerPoint slides, but this book will change what you think is really important.

José Antonio Bowen

ACKNOWLEDGMENTS

Writing a book that incorporates 50 student voices is no small undertaking. I am especially grateful to my editor, John von Knorring, for seeing the need for and value of a book that is centered on the student perspective as it relates to student engagement. His valuable insights and constant push to ensure the voices of marginalized student populations were heard helped strengthen and shape this book. I am also grateful to my faculty colleagues across the United States and in Canada, some of whom I know very well and others who jumped in to assist when they saw a call for student stories on a national electronic mailing list. Without these colleagues who share my commitment to improving the student learning experience and passion for bringing the student voice to conversations about student engagement, this book would not have been possible. This book represents a collected effort among educators across the nation who identified students and encouraged them to share their stories.

The inspiration for this book came from the last faculty development event I organized at Middlesex County College as the director of the Center for the Enrichment of Learning and Teaching before I took on a new position as associate professor in a newly established EdD program in community college leadership at New Jersey City University. At this event, a panel of community college students shared tips with faculty on how to best support their students. I, along with all the faculty in the room, were captivated by the student stories. Their stories and suggestions gave us a window into our classrooms from the student view. Hearing their varied, important perspectives shed light on how our actions, small and big, are interpreted by students. After the student panel was finished, faculty formed a long line to further engage with the student panelists. They wanted to hear more. This is when I realized there was a need for a book that centered on student stories.

I am very fortunate to be an educator. It is incredibly rewarding work. For the past 20 years, my students at the community college and graduate level have inspired me each and every day. I would like to thank all my students, past and current for helping me become a better educator. Of course, I am most grateful to the undergraduate and graduate students who were willing to share their stories and perspectives. The student contributors shared incredibly powerful stories of engagement and provided faculty with several suggestions and tips that I am sure will be helpful to readers. The stories shared throughout this book will undoubtedly serve as a reminder that our daily actions impact our students in significant, long-lasting ways and motivate us to continually improve our craft. It was truly an honor to work with so many students who wanted to give back and share their story in hopes that it would inspire faculty to use the strategies and approaches they found especially engaging.

A project of this magnitude is time-consuming and has a lot of moving parts. I would like to thank Christine Genthe, graduate assistant in the Educational Leadership Department at New Jersey City University, for her assistance with this project. Her organizational skills and attention to detail, along with her professionalism and quick response times, were of tremendous value. I would also like to thank my colleagues for their support during this process, John Melendez in particular.

And last but certainly not least, I'd like to thank my family. My husband, Dan, is always there for me. He tolerates the endless hours I spend writing and working and will often remind me to take much-needed breaks. My two sons, Ryan and David, are also always supportive of me and the many projects I take on. My son Ryan was even a student contributor! Thank you also to my parents who have always been my cheerleaders and to my niece Ashley who is simply amazing and who inspires me every day.

Thank You to the Student Contributors

Samantha Alger-Feser, University of Wisconsin, Green Bay
Jaclyn Bonacorda, University of Central Florida
Joseph Bonacorda, University of Delaware
Rosemary Brockett, Wilfrid Laurier University
Joshua Allen Brown, Kennesaw State University
Serena Rose Arandia, California State University, Stanislaus
Christina Christodoulou, Drew University
Michael Daidone, College of the Holy Cross
Kaitlynn Ely, Muhlenberg College
Amanda Galazzo, Kean University
Laura Goldfarb, Wilfrid Laurier University
Tyler Goslin, Monmouth University
Kristi Gundhus, Azusa Pacific University
Carrie Hachadurian, Western Carolina University
Amy Hankins, New Jersey City University
Ryan Harrington, Quinnipiac University
Sarah Harvey, Stockton University

Madison Hilton, Kennesaw State University
Shadiquah Hordge, New Jersey City University
Brett Hurst, The University of Alabama at Birmingham
Sara Idol, Wichita State University
Kara Infelise, Gateway Technical College
Eric Imlach, Daytona State College
Genevieve Jaser, Southern Connecticut State University
Kayla Jasper, Temple University
Cayleigh Keenan, William Paterson University
Annie Kelly, Loyola University Chicago
Sarah Lyman Kravits, Rutgers University, New Brunswick
Alison Larsen, University of Maryland, Baltimore County
Edwin S. Lee, San Jose State University
Danielle V. Lewis, University at Buffalo
David Lont, Western Michigan University
Claire Maloney, Waubonsee Community College
Wm. Dean Martin, Western Carolina University
Caleb E. Morris, University of South Carolina
Vidish Parikh, Wilfrid Laurier University
Julie Bechtel Patino, New Jersey City University
Kristina M. Perrelli, University of Rhode Island
Robert J. Portella, Rutgers University
Jessica M. Robbins, The University of Alabama at Birmingham
Amalia Carmencita Rodas, California State University, Chico
Benjamin Sackler, College of Charleston
Aditya Shah, Princeton University
Turner Smith, Kennesaw State University
Elena St. Amour, Drew University
Erin Stern, Worcester State University
Rosalyn Stoa, University of Wisconsin, Green Bay
Kayla Wathen, Middlesex County College
Michaela White, Worcester State University
Davis Wilson, Western Carolina University

S tudent engagement matters. Research has consistently shown strong
connections between high levels of student engagement and increased
academic achievement. McClenney et al. (2007) noted,

> The findings from 20 years of research on undergraduate education have
> been unequivocal: The more actively engaged students are—with college
> faculty and staff, with other students, and with the subject matter they
> study—the more likely they are to learn, to stick with their studies, and to
> attain their academic goals. (p. 1)

This was illustrated in a recent study by Delfino (2019), where student
behavioral, cognitive, and emotional engagement were all linked with
academic achievement. Kuh et al. (2007) noted that positive effects related to
student engagement were evident even after controlling for precollege variables such as ACT and SAT scores. Thus, engaging students is an excellent
way to increase student learning and overall success.

Recognizing the complexity and multidimensionality of engagement,
Lei et al. (2018) identified three primary dimensions of student engagement. The first, *behavioral engagement*, is defined as the student's level of
participation in their learning. *Emotional engagement*, the second dimension,
is defined as a student's emotional reaction to learning and to others in the
learning environment. Level of interest or boredom, feelings such as happi-
ness or anxiety, and sense of belonging all relate to emotional engagement.
The third dimension, *cognitive engagement*, is defined by the use of cognitive
strategies such as self-regulation during the learning process. Lei et al. (2018)
conducted a meta-analysis of 69 studies with almost 200,000 students and
found moderately strong positive correlations between all three types of
student engagement and academic achievement.

To increase student success, colleges and universities make many efforts
to increase student engagement. Many of these efforts are led by student
affairs professionals and are aimed at new students. For example, orientation
programs are designed to assist students with making connections to one
another, faculty, and staff and with developing a strong sense of belonging
as a member of the college community (Chan, 2019). Although research on

new student orientation is limited, some studies, such as the one by Hollins (2009), do show that these efforts are important and make a difference in terms of academic achievement and retention.

However, results from national surveys on student engagement showed that student engagement in the classroom and with faculty can have the greatest impact on student success. In a longitudinal study with almost 10,000 community college students, McClenney et al. (2007) found that active and collaborative learning experiences were one of the best predictors of higher grades, persistence, and graduation. Although engagement early in college is particularly important, Wu (2019) found that high levels of *academic motivation*, defined as being interested in or engaged with learning, were associated with higher levels of academic achievement in all 4 years of college. The engagement strategies shared in this book will assist faculty with engaging students throughout their educational journey.

The student body at colleges and universities across the nation has become increasingly diverse in terms of race and ethnicity. According to the National Center for Education Statistics (2020), 57% of students attending 4-year public colleges or universities were White, whereas 12% were Black, 19% were Hispanic, and 8% were Asian. In 2-year public colleges, the student population was even more diverse, as evidenced by 14% of the students being Black, 26% Hispanic, and 6% Asian. Engaging all students, especially students from marginalized or underrepresented populations, is important. Based on national survey data, Kuh et al. (2007) noted that "engagement has compensatory effects on first-year grades and persistence to the second year of college at the same institution for historically underserved students" (p. 3). Specifically, students of color and students of lower ability levels benefitted the most from being engaged. Thus, when faculty intentionally engage students, these actions will not only move the needle on student success outcomes for all students but also can reduce equity gaps because of the especially important role engagement plays in the success of students from marginalized or underserved populations. This book recognizes the diversity of students that faculty are encountering in their courses and highlights engagement strategies that support success for all students, especially those from underrepresented populations. In addition to sharing research that specifically relates to underrepresented populations, the diverse students represented in the stories shared also bring a personalized perspective that can motivate and guide faculty.

Student engagement can also vary for full-time versus part-time students, traditional- versus nontraditional-aged students, and students taking face-to-face versus online classes. National survey data from both community colleges and 4-year colleges and universities showed that part-time students are less engaged than full-time students (Center for Community College Student Engagement, 2015; National Survey of Student Engagement, 2013). More specifically, part-time students were less likely to report engaging in active and collaborative learning, being challenged academically, and interacting with faculty. Because there are 6.4 million part-time students attending community colleges and 4-year institutions, comprising approximately 42% of the total undergraduate student population, these data illustrating lower levels of engagement are particularly problematic (National Center for Education Statistics, 2020).

Research has also shown a connection between engagement and learning for adult learners (Lucardie, 2014). According to the National Center for Education Statistics (2020), 10% of students attending a public 4-year college are over the age of 25. This number climbs to 21% at public 2-year colleges. Although adult students typically have higher levels of engagement than traditional students, it is still important for faculty to consider ways to engage adult learners (Rabourn et al., 2018). This may be especially true for adult online learners. The average age of a student in an online bachelor's degree program is 32 (Friedman, 2017). Data from national surveys show that online learners are also typically less engaged (National Survey of Student Engagement, 2013). According to Knowles et al. (2012), adult learners are most likely to be engaged when the goals and purposes of learning are clearly shared, individual and situational differences are considered, and core adult learning principles are applied. This book offers faculty teaching both in-person and online classes numerous strategies to engage traditional- and non-traditional-aged students from diverse backgrounds. Although many of the student examples come from students taking in-person classes, there are also numerous examples from online students, many of whom would be characterized as nontraditional students. The strategies shared can easily be adapted to fit different learning approaches and methods.

Given the importance of engaging our students, this book serves as a guide to faculty who want to make the most of key moments and opportunities by developing rapport with students and using techniques and approaches that maximize engagement and learning. For each of these occasions—such as the first day of class or giving feedback, each covered in a separate chapter—I provide not only the rationale for and evidence behind these interventions but also inspirational student stories that shine a light on how even small actions can have a significant impact on the students we serve. The personal stories shared by students remind us all that learning is a social activity and that our relationships and interactions with students really do matter. The student stories provide insight into how students react and respond to our actions and teaching approaches and how high levels of engagement translate into increased learning.

As students share what they have found motivating and stimulating, faculty who have used similar approaches will find validation for their efforts and will be reminded of the importance of these actions. It is also hoped that the student stories and suggestions, which are grounded in research, will prompt faculty to revisit strategies they may have used previously but for a variety of reasons are not currently using, modify currently used approaches, and incorporate new strategies into their current practices.

We can learn so much from hearing the thoughts, values, and perspectives of students. These stories offer real-world examples of how faculty actions can really make a difference. Although the book is centered around the student stories, readers will also discover research and theoretical support for the strategies shared. In other words, this book provides faculty with rich student examples that are grounded in and supported by research and theory. It is my hope that you will find this book to be a valuable resource, one that you return to when you need a boost or reminder that the work you do every day really does matter and can have a long-lasting impact on your students, and one that you use when you are in the midst of designing or redesigning a course you teach with increased student engagement and learning in mind. Keeping the student perspective front and center as you design and implement courses will unquestionably improve the overall student experience, increase student engagement, and lead to high levels of student achievement, especially for marginalized and underrepresented students.

Overview of This Book

This book is organized into five chapters. Chapter 1 is focused on starting positive. In this chapter, faculty will discover how impactful their actions on the first day of class really are to students. Specifically, students share stories about how their professors created a sense of belonging by getting to know them and helping them feel like a valued member of the class. Student stories also illuminate how faculty can generate excitement for the course and can help students develop a higher sense of self-efficacy through building content knowledge and skill development. Faculty readers will also be challenged to think about how to use their syllabus as an engagement tool. Student stories illustrate how transparency through clearly articulated expectations along with some opportunities for choice in the learning process are excellent ways to use the syllabus to engage and motivate students.

The focus of chapter 2 is on the importance of relationships. In this chapter, the significant role of relationships, especially the professor–student relationship, is highlighted through powerful student stories. Students share examples of how in-class activities helped them get to know their professors and peers and why this was so valuable to them. Students also openly discuss why interactions with their professors outside of class are so important and share examples of how their professors engaged them outside of class. For example, some students discuss how their professors supported them when they were faced with personal challenges while others share how their professors served as career mentors who helped them discover their passion, opened doors of opportunity, and assisted them with developing a professional network.

Teaching strategies are the focus of chapter 3. Student stories illustrate how student engagement can increase as a result of teaching and learning strategies. For example, several student stories focus on how their professor personalized the learning experience through the use of examples that directly linked to their interests and used demonstrations to show real-world connections. Students also shared numerous examples of how discussions and meaningful group projects also engaged them. Throughout this chapter, students emphasize the importance of seeing the meaning and relevance of what they are doing and the opportunities to partner with peers in productive ways.

Chapter 4 highlights how meaningful assignments play an important role in student engagement. Students want opportunities to learn in authentic and challenging ways. Some stories in this chapter focus on how assignments helped them build foundational knowledge and increased their self-efficacy, while others focus on assignments that had immediate value, served a purpose, and fostered their creativity. Students really appreciated opportunities to create work products that would serve community partners and that pushed them outside their comfort zone.

The focus of chapter 5 is feedback. Student stories in this chapter focus on how learning through feedback increases their engagement and leads to long-lasting learning. Several students emphasized the value of formative assessments that were linked to summative assignments, noting that this allowed them to immediately use feedback to improve and learn. In addition to finding value in feedback provided by their professor, several students also shared how peer feedback opportunities were especially helpful and engaging. Having the opportunity to revise work after peer or instructor feedback was the focus of several other student stories. In these stories, students talked about how these opportunities communicated to them that their professor believed in their ability to improve and perform better and how engaging in the revision process led to improved products and confidence. Finally, several students focused on how even high-achieving students need and benefit from feedback.

Although faculty will likely engage in reflection as they read each chapter, there is an opportunity at the end of each chapter to engage in deeper reflection. Faculty reflection questions stem from the ideas presented in the student stories. These questions can serve as excellent independent reflection tools or perhaps could be even more effective if used as part of faculty learning communities where faculty come together with the goal of increasing student engagement.

Overview of Student Contributors

There are numerous resources on student engagement that can be helpful to faculty, but most of these resources neglect to include the student voice. The aim of this book was to bring the student voice front and center in conversations about how to engage students in the learning process. Faculty will undoubtedly find value in the insightful stories shared by students throughout this book. Anchored in research and theory on student engagement, these student stories bring a personalized perspective that makes theory and research come to life and provide real-world examples of how our actions influence the learning process. In addition to sharing their own experiences, student contributors also share suggestions and tips for faculty who want to engage and motivate students.

A total of 50 students from diverse backgrounds served as contributors. The stories shared throughout the book highlight the experiences of first-generation students, students from marginalized or underrepresented groups, nontraditional-aged students, and traditional students. Many student contributors are managing multiple roles as students, employees, and parents or caretakers.

Both undergraduate and graduate students are represented. Stories from 31 undergraduate student contributors and 19 contributors who are enrolled in master's- or doctoral-level graduate programs are shared. While many of the examples are drawn from traditional face-to-face courses—and identified as such—the majority of the ideas in the book can be transposed from face-to-face to online learning environments. Eight of the stories come from students taking online courses or who are in online programs, providing specific examples of how faculty can engage students in the virtual learning environment. Not surprisingly, as it is easier for faculty and students to connect in smaller classes and engagement is, therefore, more likely, many of the stories come from students enrolled in *small courses*, defined as fewer than 40 students. However, there are also 11 student examples from students in midsized (40–100 students) or large courses (over 100 students).

Geographically, stories come from the United States, with 19 states being represented, and Canada. A total of 39 institutions are represented. Student contributors share their experiences at community colleges; technical schools; and public and private colleges and universities, including an Ivy League school.

Dive in and enjoy the stories and strategy suggestions. Hearing the examples and suggestions shared by this diverse group of students will most certainly inspire and motivate you to reflect on your current practices and the actions you can take to increase student engagement. After engaging in personal reflection, connect with students and colleagues at your institutions and engage in deep conversations about how faculty can increase student engagement.

I

STARTING POSITIVE

The First Day of Class and the Syllabus

Although there are many ways to engage students throughout the semester, early actions can play an incredibly important role in student engagement. First impressions are influential and can have a long-lasting impact. Laws et al. (2010) found that the impressions students formed on the first day of class were consistent with the impressions that students had at the end of the semester. When students have positive experiences at the start of the class, this can increase their level of engagement throughout the entire semester. Two important early opportunities that faculty can take advantage of are the first day of class and the syllabus.

Engaging Students on the First Day of Class

The first day of class is arguably the most important one as it sets the tone for the rest of the semester. Understanding the role culture plays in learning and teaching can help faculty create an inclusive learning environment where all students believe they are a valuable member of the learning community (Chávez & Longerbeam, 2016). For example, the first day of class activities can create a much-needed sense of belonging and impact the level of student engagement. This was illustrated in a quasi-experimental study conducted by McGinley and Jones (2014). They found that students who participated in a small group activity where they discussed their perceptions of the class, how the class related to their goals, which topics interested them the most, and identified questions for the instructors reported higher levels of interest in the class and perceived the instructor to be more caring than students who did not participate in this activity.

Lang (2019) noted that the first day of class can be used to accomplish three important goals. First, faculty can use activities to promote a sense of belonging. Second, get students excited about the class. Third, the first day of class is an opportunity to help students begin to develop knowledge and skills that will serve them well throughout the semester and beyond. The student stories in this chapter provide excellent examples for faculty striving to accomplish these goals.

Creating a Sense of Belonging

One of the most important and obvious ways to create a sense of belonging in the class is by getting to know your students and helping them get to know one another. "Peer and professor engagement and openness are critical because learning is a reflective and often interpersonal act that benefits from purposeful relationship building" (Chávez & Longerbeam, 2016, pp. 159–160). Knowing the names of your students and their interests and values is a great start. Icebreaker activities are also excellent ways to help students develop a sense of belonging and excitement.

Learning Student Names and Interests

Knowing the names of your students can be an extremely challenging task, especially for faculty who teach hundreds of students each semester, but it is an extremely important task nonetheless (Cuseo, 2018). Student engagement will undoubtedly increase when professors take the time to get to know their names and interests. Although faculty typically acknowledge the value of knowing the names of their students and many put forth significant effort to do so, not all faculty know the names of all their students. In a survey on community college faculty, Linksz (1990) asked if they knew student names within the first 2 weeks of the semester; only 50% of faculty surveyed indicated that they did very often, and 28% indicated often.

Faculty can use a variety of strategies to learn student's names. For instance, faculty can have students play the name game, in which each student comes up with a descriptive adjective that starts with the first letter of their name (e.g., Caring Christine). As students introduce themselves, they also repeat all the names and descriptive adjectives of students who already introduced themselves. The last person, who should be the faculty member, therefore has to say everyone's name. This game takes time to complete and is only recommended for small- to medium-sized classes, but when used, everyone will know each other's names by the end of the class session, and this can foster a strong sense of belonging in the class. Nilson (2016) noted that students in smaller classes are more likely to expect faculty to know their name and view the accomplishment of this task as evidence of caring. However, it is also important for students taking large classes to also feel a sense of belonging. Faculty teaching small and large classes can ask students to display large name cards to help them learn their names and interact more personally with students during class.

Getting to know students requires more than just learning their names. Learning the interests of students is an excellent way to create a classroom culture where every student feels connected and part of the learning community. This can be particularly important for students of color who may not immediately feel a sense of belonging. Students of color are often attending college with predominantly White faculty, and many of the examples and references in class may not be as relevant or meaningful to them. However, Chávez and Longerbeam (2016) noted that "despite these demographic disparities, faculty can reach all students when [they] understand the influence of culture in teaching and learning, [their] own cultures of origin, and the impact of [their] origins on [their] teaching" (p. 67). When faculty take the time to learn about the interests and values of the students in their class, they will be sending a powerful message to all students, including students of color, that each member of the class is important and valuable and that you as the faculty member are committed to creating a welcoming, inclusive, and personalized learning environment. In the following student story, Rosalyn describes how one of her professors learned the name and a few interesting facts about each student in her class. These actions really made a difference and increased her motivation and engagement.

Getting to Know Me
Rosalyn Stoa
Senior | Psychology and Business Administration |
University of Wisconsin, Green Bay
Course: Research Methods in Psychology (small, in-person class)

It was the first day of Research Methods in Psychology, supposedly the hardest psychology class. I walked in and took a seat and noticed right away that the professor was chatting with someone in the front row about their interests, someone he had not met before. The first thing this professor had us do was create a nameplate and write on a note card some personal information, like our name, major, minor, where we came from, what we wanted to do, a couple of fun facts about ourselves, why we were taking this class, and what we wanted to get out of it. Throughout the whole class, he kept high spirits and a smile on his face, giving us a little primer on what the class was going to be about. At the end of class, he took a picture of each of us holding our nameplates up and collected the notecards. He told us it was his goal by the next class to know each of our names. I thought for sure he was joking. I knew he had at least 100 students in all his classes. But sure enough, by the next class, he came up to me, called me by name, and asked about my second major (business), and we talked about the applications of psychology to business, as well as my involvement on the swim team (one of my fun facts).

I was incredibly impressed that this professor cared enough to know our names and interests, and even more so when I realized that he was one of the busier professors in the department. Over the course of the semester, he would reach out to certain students if an example matched their interest and would always be early to class to talk to a couple of students about their lives and interests. I felt that he really cared about me as a person. I felt more comfortable reaching out to him for help and really enjoyed the class because it felt personal. He was able to tailor the class to what he learned about us to make it relevant.

I've always been a bit of an introvert and the kind of person to try to fly under the radar, but the actions that this professor took on the first day of class inspired me to put myself out there and get involved in the department over time. Since then, I have worked with him on several research papers and other projects, and as a result I have developed a solid CV for graduate school. I have very strong relationships with much of the psychology department because he taught me that professors are just people and they are approachable.

To all faculty, I highly recommend forming relationships with your students early in the semester. Even knowing a couple of things about each student, including our names, engages us and shows us that you care about our learning and our lives outside of being a student. Just like you, we care about more than just what we are learning in class. Often, we want to establish a strong rapport with you, but may not be quite sure how. Just letting us know that you are human and you care is a strong starting point.

ᐇᗡᐇ

Icebreakers

Icebreakers are another effective strategy that can be used to create a comfortable learning environment and a sense of belonging on the first day of class. There are numerous types of icebreakers, and most are effective at helping students become at ease in the learning environment. Many faculty will ask students to introduce themselves or converse with a partner and then introduce their partner. Although this type of activity can achieve the desired goal of creating a comfortable learning space where everyone knows one another, it may be a challenging or uncomfortable task for some students.

When determining the nature of the icebreaker, cultural considerations are important. Faculty will want to be sure that the activities they use align with the cultural values of their students. For example, some students may not feel comfortable with self-disclosure. Thus, getting-to-know-you activities that require students to share personal information with others in the class may be counterproductive for students for whom this is not culturally acceptable. Faculty will want to explicitly acknowledge and celebrate various cultural backgrounds when introducing icebreakers and may opt to give students several options for participation so that they can choose an option that fits their belief and value system.

Gehlbach et al. (2016) did an interesting study that showed that when teachers and students participated in a brief activity focused on similarities, this had a positive impact on student success, especially for underrepresented students. In this experimental study, high school students and teacher participants completed a getting-to-know-you survey early in the school year. Feedback forms, which listed five things each student had in common with the teacher, were then provided to both teachers and students. To ensure that this feedback was reviewed and considered, teachers and students were asked to answer questions related to the feedback. Teachers and students in this experimental condition perceived more in common with one another than those in the control group, and students who participated in this activity outperformed their peers who did not participate in this activity, earning higher grades. This finding illustrates the value of initial activities that highlight similarities. Gehlbach et al. (2016) noted that this intervention was of particular value for underserved students because teachers reported interacting more with underserved students, and results indicated that the achievement gap was reduced. As faculty decide what type of icebreaker to use, it may be important to focus on bringing attention to similarities. For example, faculty can ask students to write down a special person in their life and why that person is so important to them, to describe three items that are meaningful to them, to describe their perfect day, or to identify a charity they believe is especially important. Although questions such as these tap into values that can and often do vary from culture to culture, similarities will also likely be evident. After students answer questions such as these, faculty can ask students to get into small groups to identify the similarities or themes, such as the importance of family and friends, that were consistent across all responses. A large group discussion can also likely illuminate the similarities across all members of the class.

Faculty can also get creative when identifying icebreaker activities. If every faculty member used the same type of icebreaker, students would likely lose interest. Different types of icebreakers can keep students engaged. For example, Baker (2012) used a classroom karaoke exercise at the end of the first day of a large class, and students responded positively, noting that it made them more relaxed and comfortable. In the example that follows, Tyler shares how his professor used a variety of icebreaker activities throughout the semester and how these activities really helped him feel comfortable in a class with a significant amount of public speaking.

Creative Icebreakers
Tyler Goslin
Junior | Accounting | Monmouth University
Course: Business Communication (small, in-person class)

In this class, the professor worked hard to make sure we all felt comfortable in the class. My professor got us talking to one another on the first day and continued this practice throughout the semester. We frequently engaged in fun activities to increase our comfort and help us get to know one another. One of my favorite activities was when we played charades. We had to step outside of our comfort zone. Another activity we did was called speed dating. In this activity, each student would go around the room and have 5 minutes to talk to other students about anything they wanted. The only rule was that you couldn't stop talking. This allowed us to get to know everyone and connect with others.

I found these activities very important especially in a communication class where a solid chunk of the grade was presentations and speeches. I am someone who gets very nervous when speaking in front of a crowd, but this class was different. I believe it was because I had met and enjoyed everyone in the class, which made it a lot easier to feel calm standing in front of the class.

Because these activities were used throughout the semester, I was always engaged in this class. I learned a lot and had a lot of fun as well. My advice to any professor who is trying to engage their students is to think outside of the box. Do icebreakers or other brief activities that are different and unique so that students are surprised and interested every day. Linking the activities back to the lesson will help students learn while connecting with others.

❧

Faculty teaching large classes in lecture hall settings may forego an icebreaker activity because it is perceived to be too time-consuming or because the task of creating a sense of belonging in this atmosphere seems impossible. Because large lecture hall classes will most likely be composed of first-year students, creating a sense of belonging can be especially important. Students who are engaged are more likely to exhibit high levels of effort and as a result will likely have higher levels of achievement (Lei et al., 2018). It is important to establish a comfortable learning atmosphere and productive patterns of behavior early in the college journey.

In the example that follows, Alison, who is currently a graduate student, recalls an experience she had in one of her first classes as an undergraduate student. She shares how a professor used an icebreaker in a large, lecture hall class and how this made her feel excited about the course and comfortable approaching the professor. Ultimately, this professor became a mentor to her and helped her discover her career goals. Examples such as this remind faculty of the value and long-lasting impact the first day of class has for students.

Large Class Introductions
Alison Larsen
Graduate student / Management of Aging Services / University of Maryland,
Baltimore County
Course: Revolutionizing Aging (large, in-person class)

On the first day of classes in my first year at the University of Maryland, Baltimore County, I arrived at my 10:00 a.m. class about 20 minutes early as I was nervous but excited for the launch of my undergraduate career. Around 9:59 a.m., a young, peppy professor, Galina Madjaroff, walks in with Starbucks in hand and immediately has everyone's attention with her humor. Professor Madjaroff walked us through the syllabus, making jokes along the way and telling us that she hopes we have fun in the course. After all the mandatory information, such as due dates and course policies, was conveyed, Professor Madjoaroff thought it was time for her to learn about the students in the class.

Although it took the rest of the class time, about 45 minutes, Professor Madjaroff had all 120 students in the room stand up, say their name, and either share a fun fact about themselves, recommend a good television show, or do a dance move for extra credit. While the students were going around saying their names, Professor Madjaroff was truly interested in what the students had to say. She would try to make a connection between herself and the student, saying that she also had been to England or that she also liked to play video games. When it came to the students doing dance moves, only a select few were brave enough to attempt it. Some people were really good at dancing, pulling out breakdancing and ballroom dancing moves, while others, like myself, chose to show off their "sprinkler" skills. Again, Professor Madjaroff was super supportive of the dancing students as well by telling them that they did a great job and sometimes even joining in.

Although this icebreaker on the first day of class was nothing new and groundbreaking, it set a fun and light tone for the rest of the course. I felt like I could go and talk to Professor Madjaroff about a grade or an assignment, even about things that were happening on campus. The icebreaker made me feel connected to the course, to Professor Madjaroff, and to the students, which made me want to participate more and be more engaged in the class. Because Professor Madjaroff took the time on the first day of class to make that connection with each student, it was my favorite class that I took as an undergraduate student.

About halfway through the course, I decided that I would apply to be an undergraduate teaching assistant for Professor Madjaroff's course. Little did I know then that 5 years later I would be a graduate teaching assistant for her while earning my master's degree in management of aging services. Thanks to Professor Madjaroff, I was able to get two undergraduate degrees, one in biological sciences and the other in psychology with a minor in management of aging services, all while gaining experience and figuring out that I wanted to do research related to Alzheimer's and dementia after I graduated. I am thankful to Professor Madjaroff because I believe that the first day of classes in my first year shaped the rest of my undergraduate years and will continue to benefit me throughout my career.

৩৵৶

Icebreakers can be particularly important in an online class. Martin and Bolliger (2018) investigated student engagement in graduate students enrolled in online courses at eight different universities and found that "students rated the icebreaker discussion as the most important engagement strategy" (p. 216). Dixon et al. (2006) investigated the value of two creative icebreakers, one that asked students to identify an actor, actress, or character they identify with and another that required students to provide three hyperlinks that provided clues about a personal interest or their profession. Results from this small-scale study on undergraduate student engagement in an online course suggest the usefulness of icebreakers in terms of developing community and supporting collaboration. Online icebreakers can go beyond traditional getting-to-know-you discussions and also get students engaged in the course material. In the following story, Robert illustrates how his professor used an icebreaker to get students engaged with one another and the syllabus. As a result of this activity, his motivation and engagement increased.

An Online Icebreaker
Robert J. Portella
Graduate student who is a working professional / Adult and Continuing Education / Rutgers University
Course: Higher Education Feedback and Assessment (small, online class)

In an online setting, it is often difficult to connect with other students, especially if there is not a live, interactive component. One online icebreaker that was particularly effective for me was when the professor asked all of us to review the syllabus and then identify one item that we were most interested in and explain why. Outside of an embedded way to get us to more carefully look at the syllabus, there arose an unexpected thread from answering why we wanted to learn more about a certain topic. We organically revealed fears we had about the class content, all for various reasons. Through the discussion post, many of us connected with one another in a way that might not have otherwise happened.

The professor also contributed to our conversations, citing various checkpoints throughout the semester that would directly address areas we were concerned about. This interaction reduced our stress greatly. Knowing that we were going to work explicitly on those areas, whether they were a lack of foundational theoretical knowledge, unexplored experiences we already had from our individual pasts, or knowing how to write critically about these topics, made us feel more comfortable. The professor was also quite targeted with her contributions to the initial discussion, reminding students that she was always available for help along the way. I believe this conversation also provided the professor with insight as to how to craft announcements that worked in tandem with the online modules. I would notice several times that she referenced our fears and swiftly allayed them so that we could work without as many self-imposed barriers.

Asking us what we were most interested in provided perhaps a safe gateway for students to discuss what fears they had. What we reveal can directly inform future conversations, producing more opportunities for students to more readily achieve the learning outcomes. Perhaps a way for the professor to add to the existing prompt of asking what we were most interested in is to also explicitly ask what our fears are about the class. Is it the reading? The writing? A final project? Or just leave the question open to elicit responses from the students, giving the class a more personalized feel. If an icebreaker is meant to connect students, why not connect them both to one another and to the content as well?

✺

Icebreakers can be especially important in the first course of a cohort-based program. One of the primary benefits of a cohort-based approach is the built-in support of peers throughout the educational journey. However, these connections can be more difficult to establish when the program is delivered online. In the following example, Amy shares how icebreaker activities at the start of her first semester, along with early assignments, in an online doctoral program helped her connect with peers and become highly engaged. Incorporating synchronous online learning experiences, especially at the start of the semester, can help students connect to one another and feel a part of the learning community.

Online Icebreaker in a Cohort Program
Amy Hankins
Graduate student who is a working professional / Community College
Leadership / New Jersey City University
Course: Community College Leadership Institute
(small, online class)

I clearly remember what it was like meeting my cohort online the first time. I had been a bit apprehensive since approximately 20 of us would be working together for 3 years, and I did not know what to expect. I had promised this program time, energy, and money, and now I was going to see who else was there. When I signed on to our synchronous welcome meeting, the energy was already positive! There were lots of smiles, good questions, and our two leaders there as guides. During this meeting, we introduced ourselves, learned about the program expectations, and had our questions answered.

This meeting was just the first step though. Our professors strategically designed one of the first assignments to help us further connect with our peers. This assignment was essentially a paper about our goals and what ultimately led us to the program. It could have been an independent project, but instead we were assigned two partners, and the three of us had to meet synchronously in an online meeting room to provide peer reflection and feedback. I found my group members kind and funny. It eased some of the nervousness I had, and the peer review was excellent in pushing me out of my comfort zone.

As an inherently shy person, this peer review experience was invaluable. I already had true connections with some of my peers. The camaraderie and support that had been established by meaningful online interaction blew me away. I remember sitting in meetings with my peers and thinking I had finally found my people. I was looking at an exceptionally diverse group of individuals, and I felt valued and respected. It was a powerful experience.

To feel secure to ask questions, express doubt or lack of knowledge, question others, push back against ideologies, and collaborate with others is central to the learning process. To be a member of a cohort that feels like a cohesive team is special indeed, and this commitment to my new friends will help me through hard times that I expect will come over our 3 intense years of study together. I found immense value in the icebreaker activities and assignments we were given at the onset of our program that allowed us to get to know each other in meaningful ways.

〜〜

Generating Excitement

In addition to creating a comfortable learning atmosphere on the first day of class, it is also important for faculty to generate excitement about the course. Getting students enthusiastic about the course material typically results in students putting forth higher levels of effort. One of the easiest ways to get students eager to learn is for faculty to show and discuss their excitement and passion. When faculty bring a high level of energy and enthusiasm to the class, this can be contagious. Student energy often mirrors that of the faculty member.

Faculty can also get students excited about the course by incorporating fun learning activities into the curriculum. Research shows that being excited and having fun can increase student engagement. Lucardie (2014) investigated the impact of fun and enjoyment in adult learning. Adult students in this study reported that having fun in class through activities and interactions increased their motivation to attend class and learn.

In the following example, Eric, an adult student who had not been in a classroom for almost 20 years, highlights how a professor's enthusiasm and passion, along with an activity for students to get to know one another, elevated his interest in the course. As a result, he was motivated and eager to participate.

Sharing Your Enthusiasm and Passion
Eric Imlach
Adult first-year student who is a recovering addict / Social Science / Daytona State College
Course: Writing With Research (small, hybrid class)

After not being in a classroom for over 20 years, I had no idea what to anticipate on that first day. I was enrolled in the required communication core class, Writing With Research. This was an accelerated hybrid class taught by Professor Liz Barnes. Anxious and eager to make a respectable first impression, I arrived early on that first day, claimed a seat in front, and waited for the classroom to fill in.

The class was scheduled to begin in 20 minutes, and as other students arrived, I couldn't help but notice how people rarely acknowledged each other. Most either came into class affixed to their phones or retrieved them once they found a vacant seat and settled in. With most students scrolling through their devices, the energy in the classroom seemed stagnant, almost uncomfortable. Once Professor Barnes entered the room, that quickly changed.

The enthusiasm and liveliness exhibited by Professor Barnes were both apparent and rapidly contagious. She was clearly prepared and ready to take the stage. Although I may have been slightly biased because this was a course I expected to do well in, the energy she displayed made me want to pay attention and become engaged. As the class discussed the syllabus on that first day, the positive attitude and the obvious passion Professor Barnes had for the subject material made all the difference in setting the tone for the semester ahead.

After the syllabus was reviewed, Professor Barnes engaged the class with an activity that allowed students to meet each other. In a writing class that relies heavily on interaction and the peer review process, this endeavor was really important. The engagement strategy was simple. Professor Barnes asked students to determine questions that would be appropriate to ask when meeting someone for the first time. The questions the class agreed on were basic and not overly personal. For example, some of the questions we used were "Where are you from?" "What are your hobbies?" and "What is your major?" Professor Barnes then divided the class into groups and we each asked another person these questions. After we were through, our goal was to introduce that student to the rest of the class. As we made the introductions, Professor Barnes enhanced the dialogue and created conversation. This exercise ultimately established a comfortable and relaxed classroom environment. As our curriculum progressed, I felt comfortable and confident when I offered constructive criticism to one of my peers.

In my opinion, setting the tone on that first day is crucial when establishing a rapport with students. If, on that first day, Professor Barnes had arrived to class unprepared or unenthusiastic, I likely would have discredited her as a competent educator. First impressions are essential for professors and students alike. I think that when a professor enters a classroom with energy and zeal, students are attracted to that. To me, an enthusiastic class is a quintessential learning environment from which I am always most successful.

❧

Faculty can also generate excitement in students by making the course material relevant and personally meaningful. There is strong theoretical and research support that shows the connection among relevance, motivation, and learning (Priniski et al., 2018). As college classrooms become increasingly diverse, the importance of ensuring that the course content and examples are relevant to all students, including underrepresented students who are typically taught by White professors, cannot be overstated (Chávez & Longerbeam, 2016). It is critical that students of color immediately see the meaning and relevance of the course content. Faculty are best equipped to identify culturally relevant examples when they know their students.

Illuminating the relevance of course content on the first day can increase student engagement and motivation. One way faculty can do this is by inviting students to share their thoughts about the relevance of the course. Robinson (2019) found that student engagement was higher for students who were asked to write an anonymous question about psychology and engage in a discussion versus students who participated in a discussion that was guided by instructor-generated questions. This research suggests that student engagement can be enhanced when students are active participants in the learning experience from the start. Giving students the opportunity to bring their questions and perspectives into the conversation on day one gives everyone a voice and enables the faculty member to gain valuable insights about the interests of their students.

In the following student example, Aditya illustrates how a faculty member used a first-day-of-class activity to get students excited about the subject matter and course. His professor gathered personally relevant data from students so that the data could later be used in statistical examples. In addition to this activity piquing his interest because it was a unique first-day-of-class experience, this activity enabled the professor to use personally relevant data in examples throughout the semester. Students are more likely to be engaged when they are personally invested and see the relevance or meaning of the learning tasks.

Engaging Student Survey
Aditya Shah
Junior | Economics | Princeton University
Course: Statistics and Data Analysis for Economics (large, in-person class)

When I stepped into my statistics lecture on the first day of class, I was expecting to simply go through the syllabus, review the grading and attendance policy, and perhaps get a brief taste of the semester's content. To my surprise, however, my professor began class by quickly introducing himself and putting up a link on the projector. He told us to take out our electronic devices, go to the link projected on the screen, and take 5 to 10 minutes to complete the anonymous survey.

My initial thoughts when hearing this were that perhaps my professor just wanted to take care of some administrative tasks and he needed to keep us busy. Upon opening the link, however, I saw that it was an interesting survey asking me a variety of questions, including questions such as "What is your height?" and "How many siblings do you have?" as well as asking for predictions such as "Guess what the average SAT score is in this class." I was a little confused when taking the survey but nonetheless was engaged as I wanted to understand why my professor was asking me these questions.

Once everyone had completed the survey, my professor proceeded to explain that these questions were meant to gather data from a sample, which was our lecture, and that the data collected would be used throughout the semester when crafting examples for each topic. For instance, my professor used the data on our siblings to illustrate the law of large numbers, he plotted our parents' heights versus our own heights to highlight the difference between predictions and causal inference, and he used data on our age and siblings' ages to explain the difference between correlation and causation.

I found my professor's idea of using a survey engaging for two reasons. First, in statistics, we often use data on samples to make claims about the greater population. However, most of the examples used in classes often come from abstract samples and populations with which students cannot relate. By including me in the sample, I felt a more personal tie to the examples, the results, and the concepts I learned. Second, my professor's activity was engaging because it was so different from all my other first-day-of-class lectures. By doing something that didn't involve a routine overview of the syllabus for the course, I immediately became curious and thus engaged in the lecture.

For faculty seeking to engage their students both on the first day of class and throughout the semester, I believe that providing students with some form of ownership over the content and examples is critical. In classes where the content was too abstract and unrelatable to my own experiences, I felt disengaged and therefore was less likely to participate and pay attention in lectures. However, in classes where the professor related the examples and content to their students, such as in my statistics class, I was much more likely to stay engaged.

☙❦

Another way to get students excited to learn is to explain the why behind the learning journey. Faculty spend countless hours carefully designing their courses, linking learning activities and tasks to learning outcomes. Although the reason or rationale behind the assigned readings and tasks is obvious to faculty, these clear connections may not be immediately apparent to students. To alleviate this problem, faculty can take a few moments at the start of the semester to focus on the why of the learning tasks.

It is particularly important for faculty to share the why behind reading textbooks. Despite the importance of reading textbooks as a critical part of the learning process, many students report not reading their textbooks (Berry et al., 2011). This is problematic because reading has been linked to academic achievement. In a study by Landrum et al. (2012), increased reading completed by students was positively correlated with quiz scores and the final course grade. Getting students excited and helping them see the value of the readings can increase the amount of time that students spend on this important task and ultimately impact their success. In the following example, Kristi shares how her professor provided a detailed rationale for why the texts were selected and how this action positively impacted her.

Explaining the Why Behind Textbook Selections
Kristi Gundhus
Junior / English / Azusa Pacific University
Course: I and II Samuel (small, in-person class)

My fellow students and I were very quiet on the first day of class. It was a small class at 8:45 in the morning. We began to talk about the syllabus, and our professor pulled out a large stack of books that we were to read for the semester. This was not unexpected; we were in a Bible literacy course, I and II Samuel, and most Bible classes at the university required a large number of textbooks per course. I am used to this as an undergraduate English major, constantly reading everything from scholarly books to best-selling novels. Professor Birge discussed each book individually and told us why she had chosen the book as required reading. I recall her calling one of the textbooks delightful because of the author's humor.

Professor Birge described with excitement the unique properties of the books as well as her reason for teaching them. From the first day of class, students were encouraged to read our textbooks and to take notes. We were warned of the author's biases and challenged to read critically. Professor Birge made it clear that these textbooks were vital to our understanding of the class and we would write or be tested on all of them at some point or another. Her enthusiasm for the books fueled classroom discussion. Professor Birge explained the importance of keeping up with the readings, not only so that we may get the most out of class, but so we may also have stimulating discussions.

When reading, I found myself looking for the unique properties she described to us on the first day of class. I felt like I had a much better understanding as to what to look for in each book as I read them. I never had to wonder which book I got a certain concept from because I understood each textbook's unique voice enough to separate them in my mind. I felt excited for the weekly readings, some of course more than others.

I encourage educators to be passionate about what they are doing and to ask themselves why they chose the textbooks that they did. Professor Birge's warmth and enthusiasm brought a lot of people out of their shells and helped them better participate. For educators who do not choose which textbooks they teach, I suggest that you find the key aspects of the reading and guide students on what to look out for. Professor Birge found the strengths and weaknesses of our textbooks and shared this information with us. I encourage other educators to share their reasons for choosing the required readings.

Developing Knowledge and Skills

In addition to helping students feel a sense of belonging and excitement, another goal of the first day of class is to help students develop course-related knowledge and skills. Diving into the course content and skill development on day one helps students see the value of the course and gives students an opportunity to gain confidence. Students are eager to discover what the course entails.

On the first day of class, faculty can introduce the big ideas that will be discussed throughout the semester. In other words, the first day is a perfect opportunity to begin to explore the major theories or concepts of the course. These big ideas can serve as an organizational framework for the course. Because students are novice learners, they will often struggle with differentiating the important from the less important concepts (Hrepic et al., 2003). As experts in the discipline, the big ideas of the course and discipline are obvious. Faculty can use their expertise to bring attention to the big ideas and help students focus their attention on the most important concepts and skills.

In the following example, Samantha shares how her professor skillfully highlighted the big ideas in the field and course to help students see the value and importance of the course. The professor drew attention to the most important concepts by sharing several final exam questions that focused on these big ideas. In addition, the professor encouraged students to engage with the course content outside of the class by using social media for academic purposes. This helped students such as Samantha focus on not only the big ideas of the course but also the current issues in the field. As a result of these actions, Samantha had high levels of engagement in and outside of the classroom throughout the entire semester.

Previewing Final Exam Questions and Using Social Media
Samantha Alger-Feser
Commuter graduate student | Psychology | University of Wisconsin, Green Bay
Course: Abnormal Psychology (small, in-person class)

My first day of Abnormal Psychology was indeed abnormal. Professor Ryan Martin distributed his syllabus to the class. While we were going through the syllabus, he gave us his Twitter handle, as well as a few other psychologists he advised we follow. He shared his podcasts *All the Rage* and *Psychology and Stuff* and encouraged us to check them out. He also suggested we download the university's psychology app on our phones, as it had information about professors' office hours, job opportunities, internships, and psychology-related events.

By sharing his Twitter handle, podcasts, and app with us, Professor Martin engaged students in a relatable way. This kept Abnormal Psychology on my mind even when I wasn't in class. I, like many other students, would scroll through mindless Twitter content between classes, but after following a few psychology accounts, the content I was exposed to was no longer mindless. It integrated psychology into my daily routine. I would listen to podcast episodes on my way to class some mornings. I learned about the psychology of anger and some helpful study tips, and I was up to date on the latest research articles in the field. I began to follow other professor's social media accounts, websites, and podcasts. It opened up a door to a world that I did not know existed. It reframed my use of social media as well. I used social media primarily for entertainment prior to taking Professor Martin's class, but in the end it became an important piece of my academic career. Professor Martin created an opportunity for students to immerse themselves in not only Abnormal Psychology content but also the psychology community as a whole.

After we finished going through the syllabus, I assumed we would jump right into chapter 1, but instead we went over some questions that would be on the final exam. First, Professor Martin discussed how each definition of *mental health* was not merely ambiguous but actually quite different from one another. Then he went through the following list of four questions:

1. What does it mean to be "mentally ill?"
2. What forces shape our definition of mental illness?
3. In what way does American society cause (or at least exacerbate) mental illness?
4. What does it mean to be "mentally healthy?"

Learning what kinds of questions would be on the exam on day one helped me pay more attention in class. It allowed me to see the bigger picture. Abnormal Psychology was no longer a class where I simply learned how many criteria needed to be met in order for someone to be diagnosed with agoraphobia. It was a class where I learned about the complex history of mental health and that the definition of *mental illness* has yet to be perfected.

It is important for professors to find a relatable platform to interact with students. Whether through social media, personal experiences, or current examples, students will pay more attention when professors present content that relates directly to their lives. Introducing students to the major questions or ideas in the field on day one can help us get engaged.

❧

One of the most important ways that the big ideas in a course come alive is through the learning tasks. On the first day of class, faculty can get students excited about the major assignments they will be completing by sharing the rationale and explicitly making connections between the big ideas, learning outcomes, and assignments. When students see the value of tasks, they are more likely to be engaged and motivated. This is what happened to Amanda. In the following example, Amanda talks about how her professor got her engaged on day one by describing a semester-long assignment that had real-world value and application.

Getting Students Excited About a Semester-Long Project
Amanda Galazzo
Graduate student | Master of Public Administration |
Kean University
Course: Managing Information Systems in Public Administration
(small, in-person class)

I was really excited about a semester-long assignment that was clearly outlined in the syllabus. The assignment provided me with the opportunity to take lessons discussed each week in class and apply them to real-life situations. When the assignment was introduced on the first day of class, I was instantly intrigued by how relevant the task was going to be to my workplace. The professor explained the value of what we would be doing in the classroom as well as in our workplace. I was eager to begin the project and apply the skills I learned from the course to my day-to-day life.

The assignment was motivating because it let me take a deeper dive into a process at my workplace and learn a new skill of using Microsoft Access. For my project, I converted completed student surveys that were filled out after each of our department's workshops into Microsoft Access for analysis and data reporting. I was able to identify a problem at my workplace, utilize the skills I had learned from this course, and apply those skills to solve this real-life problem. This not only made the course easier to understand but most importantly made the assignment more personal than if it were just discussed in theory.

My advice for faculty on the first day of class would be to find a way to help students see that the lessons and assignments are relevant and will be of value. I have found that I am more invested and motivated if I am able to relate the course material to my life or my work. I understand it better, process it better, and am more engaged when I can say "Hey, this actually applies to me" rather than "This is just another concept or topic I am required to learn and will probably never have to use it again." The professor clearly explained the assignment and the value of this assignment in the real world.

⚬⚬⚬

The first day of class can and should go beyond introductions. Diving into the course content is also important. The first day can be used to teach students knowledge and skills aligned with the course learning outcomes. According to the expectancy-value theory of academic motivation, students will have the highest levels of motivation when they believe in their ability to successfully complete a task and perceive the task to be valuable (Wigfield & Eccles, 2000). Self-efficacy or one's belief in their ability to successfully complete a task increases through successful experiences.

The first-day-of-class activities can be designed to promote self-efficacy. Students who walk out of the first day of class having learned course content and skills will be more likely to believe in their ability to be successful in the course. Often, the course content is unfamiliar, and students may be uncertain about their ability to do well. Carefully planning the first-day-of-class lesson that helps students begin to develop essential foundational skills related to the course can immediately increase self-efficacy and motivation.

In the following example, Cayleigh shares how a professor engaged students with the course content and one another through a problem-solving activity on the first day of class. This example highlights how the first-day-of-class activity can be used to accomplish several important goals. First, students had an opportunity to practice developing course-related skills and thus build their self-efficacy. Second, students became oriented with a task, peer feedback, that they would be engaging in throughout the semester and thus immediately saw the value of this learning task. Finally, the interactive nature of the activity enabled students to start to get to know one another and develop a sense of community in the classroom.

Solving Complicated Math Problems on Day One
Cayleigh Keenan
Senior / Elementary Education /
William Paterson University
Course: Math Methods and Assessment K–6 (small, in-person class)

The first day of a college course is normally a long, drawn-out reading of the syllabus. However, in my Math Methods and Assessment class, we were immediately engaged with the course content. This course involved exploring different methods of solving mathematical problems and unique ways to assess students on the skills they learn in the classroom.

To engage us, my professor immediately gave us a problem to solve known as the handshake problem (Connelly, 2014). The problem was worded as follows: "Ryhanna is having a party. There are exactly six people at the party (including her). Every person shakes hands with each person at the party one time. How many handshakes take place at the party? Explain how you know using manipulatives, words, and pictures." We were then instructed to begin solving the problem. After 10 minutes, the professor handed out small slips of paper with different emotions and told us to indicate the emotions we were feeling while solving the problem. This was repeated approximately 10 minutes later. After around 20 minutes had passed, we were told to discuss our methods with a partner and compare our answers to check the validity of our problem-solving method. With our partners, we then presented our work to the class and had a discussion on each unique method that was used by the class.

Having to think through a variety of thought processes made this lesson so engaging. There were several methods my classmates used that I had not thought of using. This lesson helped me learn the different ways minds can approach mathematics and how collaboration in checking students' solutions to problems can be useful. In addition, the lesson kept me motivated to continue exploring multiple problem-solving strategies to improve my own understanding of mathematical content. It was also engaging to see the different emotions people were feeling during the problem-solving process. It taught me that being frustrated with a math problem can be beneficial as long as the problem is creating a productive struggle.

For faculty looking to create a more engaging classroom environment on the first day of class, I suggest finding an activity that touches on the big ideas you wish to cover in your course to give the students an overview of what is in store for them. You want to create curiosity in your students so that they keep coming back to your class hungry to learn more.

ॐ

The student examples shared throughout this chapter illustrate the value of the first-day-of-class activities. Student experiences on day one shape their perception of the course and impact their level of motivation and engagement. Faculty can strategically plan the first day of class activities with the goals of creating a comfortable learning environment, igniting excitement about the course, and beginning to help students develop key skills and learn essential content. Faculty are encouraged to learn their student's names, get to know their students and help them get to know one another through culturally appropriate icebreakers, and dive into the big ideas of the course on the first day.

Using the Syllabus as an Engagement Tool

The syllabus is an underutilized tool that can be used to motivate students by clearly articulating expectations and learning goals and mapping out the path for success in the course (Harrington & Thomas, 2018). Connecting learning tasks to learning goals shows the relevancy and meaning behind assignments and activities. Knowing the why or rationale behind tasks can increase student engagement and motivation (Steingut et al., 2017). Chávez and Longerbeam (2016) encourage faculty to reflect on the messages being sent via the syllabus to determine whether we are supporting students from all cultural backgrounds. For example, will students see themselves in the curriculum and readings? Will students have the opportunity to build on their strengths through a variety of learning tasks? What type of support and guidance is being provided?

Students appreciate it when faculty take the time to create a well-organized syllabus with detailed information about what needs to be completed and the timetable for doing so. In a study conducted by Harrington and Gabert-Quillen (2015), 66% of students indicated that they would prefer a longer syllabus that included detailed information about assignments. Students in this study who reviewed a medium syllabus (9 pages) or long syllabus (15 pages), as compared to a short syllabus (6 pages), perceived the professor to be more caring, helpful, and motivated. Although Lightner and Benander (2018) found that students appreciated brevity in the syllabus, they also found that students valued clarity in the syllabus. Thus, providing clear explanations of assignments and other pertinent class information in the syllabus can serve as a motivator for students. Students find it helpful when faculty are transparent about their expectations, taking the guess work out for students. Because faculty are experts and the ones determining the learning tasks, the connections between outcomes and assignments seem obvious to them, but students may not always connect these dots or fully understand expectations without clear explanations. Being transparent sets the stage for student success. In the following example, Michael illustrates how much he appreciated a detailed outline of course expectations along with specified due dates.

Transparent, Clear Expectations in the Syllabus
Michael Daidone
Senior / Chemistry / College of the Holy Cross
Course: Quantum Mechanics (small, in-person class)

My junior year of college presented itself as the most challenging, having to take several of the most difficult classes required in my major, one of which, quantum mechanics, carried the reputation of being the hardest class in college. However, this course had one of the best syllabi, and this made it less formidable. A common theme among college professors is to review their syllabus on the first day of class, going over the expectations, how many exams there will be, and the grading scheme. Several of my professors used what I will call an ever-adapting syllabus, in which there was never a clear date in the entire document. This allowed professors the flexibility to cover the material instead of sticking to a predefined list. However, due dates for assignments and dates for exams were not clear.

My semester in quantum mechanics started off on a different tone: Every single assignment was laid out, the date of each topic being covered was clearly labeled, and the syllabus presented links to additional resources. The syllabus was immaculately organized. This, for me, demonstrated the standards that the professor expected. Sharing clear expectations is key to engaging students on the first day. If a professor presents an incomplete and vague, unspecific syllabus on the first day of the class, they are destined to get a similar lack of effort from students in their assignments. For a professor to truly have a successful class and motivate their students, I believe it should begin with a clear and descriptive syllabus that outlines the entirety of the semester ahead.

⚭

As Michael described, students form impressions about the professor and the class based on the syllabus. Providing students with a syllabus that clearly outlines expectations, learning experiences, and tasks is critically important. Faculty can also share their teaching style and passion for the discipline in the syllabus. This is a great way for students to see the value of the course. For example, faculty can explicitly share why this course is valuable in various careers and what they find most fascinating about the course material.

Faculty can also use the syllabus to share their personality and start to develop a professor–student relationship. Because the syllabus is a document that is created by faculty for students, it should be personalized. The way in which faculty describe the learning activities, assignments, and policies will provide students with information about the professor. Students appreciate it when faculty use a positive, warm tone in the syllabus (Harnish & Bridges, 2011; Lightner & Benander, 2018). Students will often assess how much a professor cares by reviewing the messages sent via the syllabus. Students are much more likely to be engaged when they believe that their professor cares about their success. In the following student story, Madison shares how her professor used a hidden bonus in the syllabus, along with clear expectations, to engage students. This easy-to-implement strategy helped Madison see that her professor was interested in her and her success.

Hidden Bonus
Madison Hilton
Senior | Mathematics Education | Kennesaw State University
Course: Classroom Management (small, in-person class)

The professor engaged me and my classmates through a hidden bonus in the syllabus. It is a requirement for faculty to include a "plagiarism policy" section in their syllabus; a standard one to two pages of the definition and consequences of plagiarism usually comprise this portion of the syllabus. In this section, my professor added an easy opportunity for us to receive one point toward our final grade for the class.

Between two detailed sentences of the definition of plagiarism at our university, my professor added the following statement: *To prove to me that you have read this, email me a picture of something fun you did or a picture of a dog you met over the summer. Or any picture of a dog that you think is cute. If you do this before the end of the first week, you will receive a bonus point toward your final overall grade.*

This strategy was engaging because it set up the overall tone of the classroom environment, and the syllabus was sent to us prior to the first class. It also allowed me to get to know my professor's personality before interacting with her face-to-face. The strategy encouraged me to learn and stay motivated because I was engaged in reading all other discussion posts and assignment directions posted by my professor. She effectively set up an atmosphere for the classroom that was relatable and relaxed; she created an open environment where we (the students) felt as if we could share our funny and frustrating student teaching experiences. The professor always emphasized how she wanted our reflections and assignments to be more like conversations rather than formal essays. This emphasis on our writing style was supported through her initial written "addition" to a very formal section of the syllabus. The clear expectations of our writing were set from the moment the syllabus was posted onto the online platform; clear expectations helped me stay motivated and interested in the coursework.

To engage students through the syllabus and the first day of class, allow your students to show their type of work ethic, such as thoroughly reading the syllabus through hidden bonuses. This strategy also engages students by revealing a bit about your personality or common interests such as animals. Depending on the task required from the "syllabus bonus," you can set clear expectations of writing styles and expected engagement behavior as soon as possible.

༄

Another effective way that faculty can use the syllabus to motivate and engage students is by incorporating choice. Wlodkowski (2008) noted that students who have autonomy over their learning experience are often more motivated and engaged learners. Choice can be incorporated into syllabi and the course in a variety of ways. Some faculty who significantly value student ownership and choice in their learning experience ask students to be cocreators of the syllabus. Although this approach is time-consuming and challenging, it can work well in some situations. For instance, a collaborative approach to designing the syllabus could work well in an education course where engaging students in determining assessments is a goal of the course. Students taking courses that primarily focus on skill development could be asked to determine the nature of the content in the course. For example, if students are expected to primarily learn oral and written communication skills, it may be appropriate for students to determine what topics or content they will be reading, writing, and speaking about in the class. In the following example, Caleb shares how a professor asked students to select assignment options and indicate their choices at the beginning of the semester.

Choosing Assignments
Caleb E. Morris
Graduate student / Higher Education and Student Affairs /
University of South Carolina
Course: Special Topics: Diversity in Higher Education (small, in-person class)

In her Diversity in Higher Education seminar, Professor Julie Rotholz engages students by allowing them to choose the assignments they are to complete for the semester. The seminar offers students the opportunity to critically examine the concept of diversity on a college campus, including different social groups that are represented (e.g., race, gender, social class, sexuality) and how student affairs educators support and meet the needs of those groups. Students had to complete 100 points worth of course assignments. An ethnographic mini study that required us to attend an event outside of our comfort zone and write a reflection paper, which was worth 20 points, was required of all students. For the other 80 points, students could choose from a list of possible assignments. This choice-based approach demonstrated that Professor Rotholz recognized that all students are different and have unique goals, wants, and needs.

On the first day of class, students completed a contract outlining which assignments they were going to complete to earn the 80 points. Professor Rotholz emailed the contract and class syllabus prior to the first class so that students could explore their options prior to class. Examples of assignments included class contributions, a major research paper, a minor research paper, a media presentation, teaching a class with the instructor, a creative product or presentation, composition of a case study, a debate with another student, curating a current events journal, writing a book review, and composing a letter to the editor or a letter to a politician. Some assignments were individual ones, and other assignments required collaboration with one or more students, but all assignments were public in that they were shared with the class as a whole, not just with the instructor. Professor Rotholz was the sole assigner of grades. This combination of student choice and public presentation is engaging because students were able to tailor their learning experience to meet their unique needs and goals. Knowing that you had to share your work with your classmates and not just the instructor is extra motivation to produce the best work possible.

A particularly engaging assignment choice was to teach a class with Professor Rotholz, which involved selecting a class to coteach, meeting individually with Professor Rotholz to create learning outcomes, designing activities and discussion questions, and brainstorming any additional readings to assign the class. This assignment engaged students because they were able to work with the instructor one on one to discuss the class topic in-depth, why that topic was relevant and important, what future student affairs educators should know about the topic, and how to teach it. Teaching forces students to really invest in a topic in a more in-depth way, and working with Professor Rotholz provided an opportunity for mentorship from an experienced instructor on how to plan and facilitate a class.

❧❧

As just described by Caleb, choice can be incredibly motivating for students. This approach enables students to build on their strengths and develop knowledge and skills related to their unique goals. However, it is important to recognize that this collaborative approach to syllabus design or significant choice with assignments is not always possible or even desirable. Determining course assignments and activities that align with course learning outcomes is challenging work that typically requires the expertise of faculty and takes significant time. If faculty give choice about different types of assignments, it is critical that all the assignment options accurately measure whether the student learning outcomes have been achieved.

Fortunately, there are many other ways to incorporate choice into the syllabus (Harrington & Thomas, 2018). Perhaps the most common strategy used for incorporating choice is allowing students to select a topic of interest for projects or assignments. Another option is to give students some choice about due dates. For example, in an online course, students could perhaps decide if it is best for module assignments to be due on Sunday or Monday and at what time of the day.

With increased pressure for assessment and accountability, many colleges and universities are shifting toward standardized syllabi with little to no choice for students. An unintended consequence of overly standardized and prescribed syllabi may be lower levels of student engagement and motivation. Faculty are encouraged to investigate the opportunities for choice in the syllabus. In the following example, Michaela shares how her professor engaged students on the first day of class by getting to know them and using their input and feedback to determine the focus of what the professor called student choice days. This is an excellent example of how faculty can maintain responsibility for the core design and structure of the course while also enabling students to feel ownership and control over some lessons.

Student Choice
Michaela White
Junior | Psychology | Worcester State University
Course: Motivation (small, in-person class)

On the first day of class, Professor Raftery-Helmer spoke to us about the material we were going to learn and how it pertained to our lives. She described her journey to becoming a professor and how she became interested in motivation. Introducing herself and describing her story personalized her and made her seem more human and less super-genius. As a result, it was less intimidating to approach and talk to her in the future.

Professor Raftery-Helmer then went around the room and had us introduce ourselves and state one interesting thing about us. While we did this, she was actively engaging with us and clearly trying hard to learn our names, showing us that she cares about who we are as people. Once introductions were finished, she went through the syllabus. The last few days were marked *student choice*. We completed an anonymous poll about which topics interested us the most. Also, as we went through the syllabus, she would ask us about certain topics and if we wanted to focus more heavily on one topic over another. She made it very clear that the syllabus would change throughout the semester based on our engagement.

These initial actions made me excited for the semester. She was autonomy supportive from the very start. She provided us with a choice about the topics we wanted to cover and how we wanted to cover them. I didn't feel restricted in what we were learning and how I went about learning the material. As a result, I found myself more focused on learning the material to learn it and not just get a grade.

On the first day of class, let students get to know you and try to get to know them. Show them that you care more about them than the grade they will get in the class and that you are there to help them succeed by making yourself available. Focus your syllabus around what they want to learn while also still being able to cover the subject matter that needs covering. Be clear about what you want from them, and then ask them to be clear about what they want from you.

ॐ

As illustrated in several student stories, the syllabus is an opportunity to motivate and engage students. As faculty create or revise their syllabi, they can consider how to engage students by clearly mapping out expectations and the rationale for assignments and other learning tasks. Faculty can also show their personality through welcome or teaching statements and the tone of the syllabus. Finally, faculty can consider how and when choice can be incorporated into the syllabus. Students will undoubtedly appreciate your efforts to engage them using the syllabus.

Faculty Reflection Questions

1. What strategies do you use to learn the names of your students and some interesting facts about them? What new strategies could you try?
2. What first-day-of-class activities have you used that promote a sense of belonging and excitement? What are some additional ways you can accomplish these goals? How might these activities be perceived by students from different cultures?
3. How do you communicate your passion and excitement for the class? What else might you do to get students excited about the course?
4. How do you bring attention to the big ideas of the class on the first day? What content and skills are you helping students develop on day one? How can you further develop skills and confidence on the first day of class?
5. How do you communicate course expectations and the why behind learning tasks on your syllabus?
6. How does your personality come through on the syllabus? How can you further personalize the syllabus so that students can get to know you and your teaching style?

7. How will your syllabus be perceived by students from underrepresented groups? How can you communicate your commitment to supporting all students?
8. What opportunities for choice are given to students in the syllabus? How can you add further opportunities for choice to increase student engagement?

2

POWER OF RELATIONSHIPS

Learning is a social activity. According to social learning theory, relationships play a powerful role in motivation and learning (Bandura & Walters, 1963). Bowen (2012) emphasized that faculty-student interactions and connections are critical to learning. Students are more likely to be engaged and put forth higher levels of effort when they feel connected to others and when they believe others care about them and are there to support them. Relationships were emphasized in Chickering and Gamson's (1987) classic work where they identified seven principles of effective undergraduate education. In this seminal work, the critical role of relationships was highlighted in the first two principles. The first principle emphasized the importance of the professor–student relationship, and the second principle focused on the value of relationships with peers and classmates.

Research has shown that positive professor–student rapport is connected to numerous positive outcomes. In a study by Wilson et al. (2010), professor–student rapport predicted student attitudes toward the course and professor, student motivation, and perceived learning. Demir et al. (2018) also found that professor–student rapport predicted student perception of the course, attendance, and perceived learning. In a study conducted by Delfino (2019), students reported that having a positive relationship with their instructor increased their confidence as a learner and encouraged them to think more critically about the subject matter.

Unfortunately, some students are more likely than others to benefit from professor–student relationships. Student-faculty rapport and academic achievement can be impacted by race, ethnicity, gender, and sexual orientation (Joyce, 2015; Rakow, 1991; Redding, 2019). Students from underrepresented groups are not as likely to have strong, positive relationships with faculty. For example, Joyce (2015) found that sexual minority youth had lower quality relationships with their teachers. More specifically, sexual minority youth were less likely to report being cared about by their teachers, were not as likely to report getting along with teachers, and were less likely to report being treated fairly by teachers. Cooper and Miness (2014) found that students of color, especially Latinx students, were less likely to share student-teacher experiences characterized by care and understanding.

On a positive note, when faculty at Oakton Community College had 15-minute meetings with every student in their course at the beginning of the semester to get to know them and find out how they can help them be successful, this resulted in higher retention rates for all students, especially for Black students. The overall persistence rate was 65.7% for students who had at least one professor who used the 15-minute meeting as compared to the 51.4% persistence rate for the overall community college student body. For Black students who had at least one faculty member who participated in the 15-minute program, the persistence rate was 60.7% as compared to an overall persistence rate of 42.2% for Black students (Supiano, 2020).

Having a teacher with the same racial or ethnic background is advantageous (Redding, 2019). The faculty body, however, does not usually represent the student body in terms of race and ethnicity. Although the diversity of faculty is on the rise, only 24% of college faculty in 2017 was non-White yet 45% of the student body was non-White (Davis & Fry, 2019). Because of this current reality, faculty will want to put forth the extra effort to get to know students who are different from them. Faculty can reach out and interact with students on an individual basis to learn about their interests and values and to provide encouragement and support (Cooper & Miness, 2014). During these initial interactions, it can be helpful to focus on similarities as this can lead to increased interactions and higher levels of achievement (Gehlbach et al., 2016).

Connecting With Students During Class

Faculty can begin to develop relationships with their students by sharing personal information about themselves. Students want to get to know their faculty. Brookfield (2015) refers to this as disclosing personhood. Faculty who share personal examples to help illustrate points or share previous academic struggles to instill hope enable students to see them as human beings rather than just professors. As a result, students will be more inclined to approach and interact with faculty.

Faculty can develop and nurture these relationships throughout the entire semester in many ways. Faculty actions before, during, and after class can pave the way for professor–student relationships to develop. Simple actions such as getting to class early or staying late to interact with students, allocating class time for conversations about how students are doing in general, and answering questions related to the course can signal to students that the professor is approachable and caring.

In an interesting study by Case (2013), students of color identified faculty from whom they felt they learned the most. The faculty members were interviewed and, in some cases, observed in the classroom. During classroom observations, the researcher saw the professor walk around the classroom and interact with students before, during, and after class. Professors also openly shared their exposure to other cultures and how these experiences had a positive impact on them and their teaching, and they also invited students to share their own experiences.

Students are most likely to connect with faculty when faculty make efforts to get to know them. In addition to knowing and using student names in class, faculty who are interested in developing professor–student relationships will also want to ask students questions about their interests and engage in actions that show that they care about their students. There are numerous approaches that faculty can use to get to know their students. In the following story, Shadiquah shares how a getting-to-know-you Pecha Kucha was used to help students connect to their professor, one another, and the course content.

Getting-to-Know-You Pecha Kucha
Shadiquah Hordge
Graduate student / Community College Leadership / New Jersey City University
Course: Community College Leadership Institute (small, in-person class)

One powerful activity that I participated in was a Pecha Kucha presentation. Pecha Kucha is a specific type of presentation where the presenter creates 20 slides composed of images, and each slide is shown for only 20 seconds. It's a fast-paced and focused presentation. We were tasked with sharing our background, cultural identity, and research interests as well as explaining how our research could have a positive impact on equity and success. We were also encouraged to reflect on our personal and professional journey and share our aspirations.

The professor connected with students by conducting the presentation herself to model the approach and help us get to know her. This joined the students to the instructor and developed an immediate bond. It made the students identify the instructor as not only a teacher but also a person. Since the Pecha Kucha presentation style was new to us, the modeling she did also helped us better understand the task.

Students were given the freedom to express themselves by incorporating childhood pictures, cultural items, and family memories as we wanted. These small tokens of expression helped us appreciate the diversity of our fellow students and created an atmosphere that was respectful of ethnic backgrounds. This activity helped us connect with one another and the professor. It also inspired us to focus on the importance of the work we would be doing in the doctoral program and how this work would really make a difference in terms of equity and social justice.

I would advise other faculty members to use activities that make way for reflection, problem-solving, information sharing, and authentic learning experiences where diversity is celebrated.

৩৩৩

Establishing relationships at the beginning of the semester is important. However, it is also important for faculty to continue to get to know their students as the semester progresses. Being together for approximately 15 weeks provides ample opportunity for relationships to develop and strengthen. For example, faculty can invite students to share their perspectives and ideas in class discussions. When students share examples and perspectives in class, faculty become more aware of student interests and values. Although discussions can be a great way to build connections, there is rarely enough time during class for everyone to participate.

Thus, it can be helpful to have online conversations. One of the primary advantages of using online conversations is that every student participates. Thus, all voices are heard. Faculty can develop relationships by responding to student comments, sharing personal examples, and communicating genuine interest and care. This information can also be used to determine meaningful examples of concepts in future lessons and as a conversation starter for outside of class meetings.

Writing assignments are another way that professors can get to know their students. Incorporating reflection opportunities that require students to make connections between the course content and their personal lives at the end of each class or week is an effective way to help professors get to know their students while also promoting learning. Reading student reflections can provide faculty with a window into the student experience in their class.

Content-specific writing can also enable faculty to get to know their students. For example, when students are given the option of topic choice, their selected topic opens a door to communication about their interests. In the following student story, Vidish, an economics major, shares how writing assignments and related discussions were used as a vehicle to foster professor–student relationships.

Using Writing to Foster Relationships
Vidish Parikh
Senior | Economics | Wilfrid Laurier University
Course: Writing and Presentations in Economics (small, in-person class)

Professor Garbati emphasized the learning opportunities that a course in economic writing presented. Economic policy writing is about creativity as much as it is about academic voice, and so this approach forces us to think broadly. We spent the semester working together—teacher and student—deconstructing what it meant to write well. She took an interest in each student's personal development in the writing journey. The emphasis was on writing as a personal journey that could be augmented through collaboration. What I found most engaging was my professor's willingness to listen to different student perspectives.

This engagement strategy was built on trust. It started from day one when the inherent subjectivity of writing was discussed. Approximately 20 minutes was taken out of each class for students to work on their personal writing journey assignment. We then engaged in a discussion with the professor about our writing progress.

This engagement strategy built a positive learning environment where I felt comfortable asking questions. It made me enthusiastic to learn the material. When a professor is invested in your academic journey, you feel empowered and believe what you are doing matters. My professor's enthusiasm and emphasis on collaboration were the motivating factors; the class became akin to a team, one that was going through a collective transformation. She focused on relationship building and not solely on the product; this served to demystify the writing process.

To engage students, clearly explain the significance of everything you are teaching. This may help students relate to your research, gain an interest in your work, and allow a professional professor–student relationship to develop. Follow-up with students who show evidence of engagement in your class for possible research assistantships or other means to engage with subject matter through mentorship opportunities. For instance, Professor Garbati noticed my genuine interest in sharing my writing journey with others. She kept me informed of opportunities to become an academic writing tutor and to speak to other students about the writing process.

꘏

Faculty can also structure class time in a way that allows for personalized interactions with individuals or small groups. For example, while the class is working in small groups on a collaborative project, professors can walk around the room and have one-on-one or small group conversations with students. Increased interactions between the professor and students on an individual or small group basis make the course more personal.

As professors gain knowledge about student interests, these interests can be incorporated into lessons throughout the semester. This personalized experience can engage students and be a foundation for growing productive professor–student relationships. In the following example, Michael, a chemistry major, discusses how a professor got to know his students and then modified his lessons to align with their student interests.

Tapping Into Student Interests
Michael Daidone
Senior | Chemistry | College of the Holy Cross
Course: Food, Power, and the Environment (small, in-person class)

For my free elective, I decided to choose a class that piqued my interest and differed from anything I'd previously experienced. The class Food, Power, and the Environment explored the history of food production, environmental impacts on food, and the food production impact on the environment. Being a health-conscious individual, I thought I'd find interest in the topic. However, unbeknownst to me before registering, the professor was the most beneficial part of the course. From the first day, he brought enthusiasm and excitement to every class. Each day he began by asking everyone how their week was going or how their weekend went. Throughout the semester, his PowerPoints, littered with fun facts and witty jokes, kept the conversation interesting and engaging.

He took the time to get to know each student during the class period. For example, he took polls of student interests on certain topics and then, the night before each class, he would adjust his PowerPoints to customize each of his lectures, ensuring the examples would be of interest to certain students or fit the majority interest.

I took an interest in organic farming, the regulations behind it, its motivation and developments, and through weekly discussions with the professor, either before or after class, he picked up on this. With each student, he attempted to find an area of interest related to the topics of the class. Subsequently, he would send you an email with an article relating to that topic and paragraphs of his own thoughts. This almost weekly email from him continuously kept me engaged in the class. By the end of my semester, I even found myself randomly reading articles online and sending them over to my professor, also sending him lengthy emails with my thoughts.

As a professor, to truly engage with students, sometimes you must extend beyond the traditional examples and play to the interests of the students. My professor that semester knew how to engage each student, simply by putting in that extra effort.

✺

Relationships can begin to develop through in-class experiences and then can strengthen with out-of-class interactions. Cuseo (2018) notes that when students have positive experiences with their professors during class, they are more likely to engage with faculty outside of the classroom. Michael's story illustrated how valuable it was for the professor to incorporate student interests into the class discussions and activities and how this set the stage for professor–student engagement outside of the classroom.

Michael's example also illuminates how email can be used to strengthen professor–student relationships that begin to develop in the classroom. Sheer and Fung (2007) found that the frequency of emails from professors, the perceived helpfulness of these emails, and promptness in replying were all related to positive professor–student relationships. The tone and nature of the email, of course, matters. In a descriptive study conducted by Dickinson (2017), students in a course where the email tone was more positive had higher pass rates than for students in a course where emails from the professor were not as positive. One of the primary differences was that the emails with a more positive tone included encouraging comments. Thus, faculty can strategically use email to begin to shift the relationship from one that only exists in the classroom to one that goes beyond the classroom walls.

Getting to know students can obviously be more challenging in large classes. Not surprisingly, research has shown that students in larger classes are less likely to connect with their professors as compared to students in smaller classes (Beattie & Thiele, 2016). Despite how challenging it can be to connect individually with students in large classes, it is important for students to feel connected in large classes, especially since students are most likely to enroll in large classes during their first year of college. Faculty teaching large classes can leverage technology and use discussion boards where students can share information about their interests and values. Although connecting with every student in a large class can seem like an impossible task, with planning this can be accomplished during the semester. Prior to each class, faculty can randomly review several student responses and reach out to students virtually or in person before or after class. Although this is a time-consuming task, it is one that students will really appreciate.

Interacting With Students Outside of Class

As with all relationships, professor–student relationships take time to develop. The time that professors and students spend together during class is important, but often not enough to develop strong professor–student relationships. There is a significant body of literature that shows the value of professor–student interactions that take place outside of the classroom. For example, national survey data have shown that student–faculty interaction was associated with higher grades and degree completion (McClenney et al., 2007). Lundberg (2014) found that student interaction with faculty was the best predictor of learning.

Meeting with students individually outside of class is an excellent way to strengthen and enhance professor–student relationships. During these meetings, faculty can get to know their students and provide words of encouragement. Because faculty are role models, encouraging words can really make a difference in terms of student success (Bowen, 2012). This can be particularly important for students who are disengaged. In the following example, Joshua, a self-described disengaged, first-generation student, shares how an individual meeting with his professor helped him become engaged. This one gesture, inviting Joshua to a conversation, really made a difference.

An Individual Meeting With a Disengaged Student
Joshua Allen Brown
First-generation senior who is employed full time / Sociology
Kennesaw State University
Course: English Composition II (small, in-person class)

In my first semester, I was taking a course that I wasn't particularly interested in, and to make matters worse, it was an early morning class. My level of engagement was effectively nonexistent, and that disengagement and lack of desire undoubtedly showed in the classroom. Although this was the case with other courses, the difference with this one was that by the end of it, I could actually tell that my professor, Professor Trivedi, genuinely cared not just about the subject matter but also about each of his students. This level of care for his students stood out enough to encourage me to be engaged strictly out of respect for him and what was then only the beginning of a professor–student relationship that continues to exist 8 years later.

Although I remember noticing smaller instances in the classroom, the first event that made me significantly more engaged came about when I missed one of our important reading quizzes near the middle of the semester because I was sick. Not having any doctor's excuse but not wanting the zero, I reached out with little expectation of being able to make it up, and he responded saying that I could come to talk to him in person. By then, most of my communication with professors were effectively negative, disappointing experiences, so I expected no less in this instance. Thankfully that was not at all the case.

When I met with him, I certainly had some sense of dread just because I would have to explain why I missed the quiz, but within moments that hesitation disappeared entirely. It was refreshing to have a professor speak with me as if they truly cared about what I was saying, and it was the first and still one of the few select occasions where I enjoyed speaking with a professor and felt positive afterward. We did not even speak much about the assignment itself. Instead, we spent most of the time discussing how college was going for me and what I made of it. After this conversation, I approached his class in a significantly more positive light simply because there was no doubt in my mind that he cared that I was getting something out of it.

Knowing then that the professor cared about me as a student engaged me to *want* to care about the course, at a time where I very well could have just checked out of it. In one aspect, I wanted to do well to repay the effort I could see him putting forth with effort of my own. In another, just trusting that what I was doing in the class had an actual purpose rather than just being done because "the instructor said so" encouraged a stronger level of engagement. If he had never asked me to meet with him in person, I could have easily dismissed even the elevated level of care I noticed he had in the class as insignificant. Instead, a few minutes of actual conversation made all the difference, and seeing he genuinely cared engaged me to do exactly the same.

⚮

Joshua's story reminds us of the importance of caring. Students are much more likely to learn when they are in a supportive, caring environment. Small actions in and outside of the classroom can really make a difference. As Joshua described, one short conversation with his professor outside of class helped him become engaged.

One-on-one meetings between professors and students are also an opportunity for students to gain confidence. As experts in the field, faculty can sometimes forget how much courage is needed to learn and engage in activities outside of one's comfort zone. Self-doubt and a lack of self-efficacy are common on college campuses. Students with higher self-efficacy are more likely to exhibit high levels of effort, set higher goals, and ultimately achieve more (Cheng & Cheou, 2010; Drago et al., 2018; Locke & Latham, 2002).

The role of self-efficacy becomes increasingly important for students who encounter challenges or failures because students are more likely to persist in these situations when they have high levels of self-efficacy (Komarraju & Nadler, 2013). Building self-efficacy for all students is important, but it is especially important for student populations that have consistently performed more poorly on academic tasks. Manzano-Sanchez et al. (2018) conducted a systematic literature review on the impact of self-efficacy on academic performance for Latinx students and found that academic self-efficacy significantly predicted academic performance. Because self-efficacy plays such an important role in academic achievement, building academic self-efficacy can be a path toward reducing or eliminating racial and ethnic achievement gaps. Faculty can provide words of encouragement and support to help students succeed on tasks.

One of the main reasons why students interact with faculty outside of class is to understand the course materials or get guidance on an assignment. It takes courage for students to acknowledge difficulties and seek help. Although office hours are the traditional avenue for students to seek support, technology tools and platforms can also be used for this purpose (Bowen, 2012). When students seek support, professors can instill hope and confidence and build relationships with students. Through these interactions, students can receive helpful feedback, gain knowledge, and develop skills that will help them successfully complete tasks. When students experience success with quizzes, exams, and other assignments, this increases their belief in their ability to successfully complete the task at hand.

In the following example, Michaela shares how much she appreciated the time her professor took talking with her outside of class and her willingness to find a time other than the scheduled office hours to have these conversations. During these meetings, Michaela was able to deepen her knowledge of course content and increase her confidence. In addition to reviewing exam content, Michaela also discussed real-world applications of the course content with the professor during these individual meetings. These conversations were really important to Michaela and increased her engagement.

Deeper Levels of Learning
Michaela White
Undergraduate student / Psychology / Worcester State University
Course: Motivation (small, in-person class)

Professor Raftery-Helmer made it clear she was available for extra help with class or any other issue we were having. On top of office hours, she let us email her to schedule appointment times to meet. This alone created the sense that this professor really cared about us as people and not just as students.

I met with my professor because I was unclear on what I did wrong on an exam and I wanted to understand how I could improve. She looked through the exam with me and understood my perspective. We discussed how I could have explained certain things better. When I demonstrated an understanding of the material, she sometimes adjusted my grade. Yet, she made it clear from the start that we should never meet with her expecting to get back points. She wanted us to work primarily on understanding the material; then she was up for a discussion if we were worried about points.

Professor Raftery-Helmer made me feel accepted and comfortable confiding in her. I never felt judged when I needed to clarify something or talk about my feelings. I met with Professor Raftery-Helmer multiple times over the semester. On several occasions, I talked with her about connections between the course material and my job. I felt frustrated that we had evidence to show how certain approaches work better over others, yet the real world was not using these approaches. Through discussing my job, I was able to make connections between it and the class, helping me learn and keeping me interested in the class.

I was not available during her office hours, so she met with me in the morning so we could discuss my job and these connections. I really appreciated the fact that she was willing to make herself available outside of her office hours. If I had asked to meet but she was only willing to meet during office hours, I would have missed out on the opportunity to discuss the course with her.

To create a strong professor–student relationship, professors need to be willing to create extra time for their students. Be like Professor Raftery-Helmer and make yourself approachable so students want to make connections between the course material and their own lives, making the information in class more interesting to learn and easier to remember. It really helped me develop a deeper understanding of the course content.

৵৵

In addition to building academic confidence, one-on-one meetings also provide students with an opportunity to discover and explore academic and career interests. According to research conducted by Greenbank and Hepworth (2008), student career decisions are often influenced by professors. During individual conversations, students can get to know their professors and gain a deeper understanding of their research interests. Students can also share their interests and discuss potential career opportunities. These personalized conversations can help students discover or clarify interests. In the following example, Jessica, a first-generation student who started her studies at a community college, discusses how meeting with her professor helped her gain confidence as a learner and discover research interests.

Gaining Confidence and Discovering Interests
Jessica M. Robbins
First-generation, graduate student who started at community college
English | The University of Alabama at Birmingham
Course: Reading/Writing/Research for Literature Students
(small, in-person class)

When I transferred from a community college to a 4-year institution in the fall of 2016, I anticipated that my professors would not take much interest in me or my work as a student. However, when I made an appointment to see my first university literature professor in her office for help on a paper, I found that this was not the case at all. She remembered my name, addressed all my questions about the assignment, offered ideas, and even asked me about my life. Although I walked in that day thinking that I would be rushed out the door, she was gracious and welcoming, which not only made me a more confident student but also caused me to become more invested in her class.

Throughout the remainder of the semester that I took her class, I made several additional appointments to see her for help, during which time she always made a point to ask me how I was doing and how all my classes were going. We even talked about things that were not related to school, including our pets and families. Although I worried about imposing on her time, she never made me feel unwelcome and talked with me about anything I happened to bring up. In addition to encouraging individual appointments, she also set aside time during each class to answer questions about assignments. Each class started with her asking what questions we had, which encouraged me to start on my work early and made me feel as if she sincerely cared that we understood our task.

Because of the efforts my professor took to get to know me, I began to see the class as an opportunity for growth as opposed to a test of my worth as a student. I felt more confident in myself knowing that she was willing to help, which caused me to be more creative and try new things with my writing. As a result of my newfound confidence, I was able to identify one of the major research interests I would end up taking with me to graduate school: animal studies theory. Had she not invited me to her office during the first semester and taken the time to ask about my personal interests, I may not have discovered this research interest. However, because she did take the time to talk to me about my concerns and my interests, this class helped me discover research interests that I would continue to pursue even after the semester ended.

For faculty who are interested in pursuing this strategy, I would say that students are more likely to put effort into a class when they feel that they are valued not only for their work but also as human beings. By taking the time to learn what students are interested in outside of the class, there is a greater chance that a professor will be able to connect the work in the class to students' lives. Students will then feel more invested in the material. Being available to answer students' questions is another way students can see that their professor cares about them and wants them to succeed. Because my professor offered so many avenues for us to receive help on our assignments, I felt that she truly valued students' individual growth and success, which caused me to want to devote more energy to the work of the class.

⚘

Assisting Students Struggling With Personal Challenges

Relationships are especially important when students face challenges. Members of a support system can be there to listen and provide encouragement and guidance when difficult situations are encountered. Academic challenges are common in college and having a positive professor–student relationship can be very helpful in these situations. In an interesting study that Micari and Pazos (2012) conducted with students taking organic chemistry, they found that "the more a student felt he or she had a positive relationship to the professor—that is, looking up to the professor, feeling comfortable approaching the professor, and feeling that the professor respects the students—the higher the student's final grade" (p. 45). Thus, positive professor–student relationships play an important role in academic success.

Academic performance challenges are sometimes due to students struggling with the cognitive tasks associated with the assignment, but in other cases it is more about fitting the academic work into their complex lives. Students today are often juggling many different roles and responsibilities. Being a student is only one part of a student's identity. Perna (2010) reported that almost half of traditional-aged college students work, many working a substantial number of hours per week. Inconsistent work schedules and work demands placed on students can interfere with student learning.

Many students also have significant family obligations. Recent survey data indicate that 22% of all undergraduate students are parents, and many are single parents (Ascend & Institute for Women's Policy Research, 2019). In addition to the typical responsibilities that come along with being a parent, many students may face unexpected issues such as childcare challenges if a child or caregiver is ill. Students may also have responsibilities related to caring for parents or siblings. These family obligations can be challenging and may impact student success in college.

Having an understanding professor in these situations can make a significant difference for students. A caring professor with a flexible late policy for assignments can help students succeed. Bombardieri (2019) reported that flexibility with assignment due dates led to improved grades for community college students, and this was particularly beneficial for Latinx students.

In addition to daily challenges, many students also face other significant issues that could easily derail their success. For example, a student may lose a loved one, be diagnosed with a disorder or disease, or experience a traumatic event. Many college students are also struggling with mental health issues (Crist, 2018). These challenging situations and experiences can significantly impact academic performance.

Research shows that having a positive mindset and a strong support system fosters resilience in these challenging scenarios (Carver, 1998; Dawson & Pooley, 2013). Based on national survey data, it was found that "personal connections are the unanticipated success factor—a critical variable that improves the odds of persistence" (Center for Community College Student Engagement, 2009, p. 3). Although faculty should not take on the role of counselor, they can help students see hope in the future and be a part of a student's support system. Students are more likely to share personal struggles and seek help when they believe their professor truly cares about them. In many cases, having someone such as a professor there during a difficult time can be what keeps a student in school. Wm. Dean, a non-traditional-aged, first-generation, low socioeconomic status student, shares how a professor being there during a personally challenging time really made a difference for him.

Dealing With Family Illness and Loss
Wm. Dean Martin
First-generation, low socioeconomic status, non-traditional-aged graduate student who is employed full time / Higher Education Student Affairs
Western Carolina University
Course: Religion, Suffering, and the Moral Imagination (small, in-person class)

During this time in my life, Professor John Whitmire took an active role in being aware and supportive of what I needed as a student and as a person to be successful in my academic pursuit. As a new student in his class, Professor Whitmire did not know me well, nor did I know him, but he was sympathetic to things going on in my personal life. He recognized how much of an impact dealing with a parent in intensive care 6 hours away and not being able to be there had on me. As the diagnosis was made and subsequently the move to hospice arranged, both Professor Whitmire and Amy McKenzie were reassuring, supportive, and intentional about reaching out via email, calls, text messages, and in person both during and after the ordeal. Upon returning from the break after my dad's death, Amy was the first person to approach me with a hug and supporting and encouraging words. I have shared with others that had it not been for Professor Whitmire, and for Amy, there is no way I would have been able to remain in classes and continue on at a place where I knew no one and had no family or friends around for support. They are also part of my inspiration for continuing my journey through graduate school.

Knowing and understanding mitigating factors in a student's life beyond the classroom is vital to understanding their classroom performance. Creating an environment that is welcoming, safe, and supportive encourages success and perseverance for students who otherwise may not be retained because of factors beyond their control.

It was difficult for me to come back into education as an adult who has worked for over 15 years and has children. Doing all of this and then having to face the death of a parent, especially one who the relationship with was not always great or existent until adult years, made this even more challenging. Understanding the different needs of students requires intentionality and getting to know students on a deeper level through engaging conversations, open-door policies, and being genuine in your comments and behaviors.

For nontraditional students and students who are from low socioeconomic backgrounds, it is often a matter of choosing which thing to address and care for first. These decisions often equate to sacrificing educational journeys, withdrawing from classes without a conversation with instructors for fear of judgment, or ceasing to go to class without any type of official action at the university level until it is too late. The extra few minutes at the start of each class spent checking in or reminding students that you are always available via email or office hours makes the difference. Being approachable and sympathetic to students' situations and offering supportive words and actions can provide the motivation and sense of belonging needed to stay in school. Take the time; be human; have deep, non-academic conversations with students; and invest in them even if you think they are only with you for a semester.

❧

Faculty are best positioned to know when a student may be struggling with a personal issue. Students struggling with personal or health issues may miss class, submit assignments late, be more tired, experience changes in weight, or have significant changes in mood or other behaviors. Faculty, especially those who know their students, can often pick up on these signs and symptoms and can encourage students to utilize on- or off-campus supports. In the following student example, Amalia describes how important it was to her to have a professor who cared enough to connect her to counseling resources on campus.

Mental Health Referral
Amalia Carmencita Rodas
First-generation Latina / Master of Public Administration
California State University, Chico
Course: Peer Mentor Training (small, in-person class)

I am the eldest child in my family and was born in Guatemala in a small village called San Pedro Soloma. My maternal grandmother only spoke our native language, Q'anjob'al, and my mother fully learned Spanish after we had migrated to California. Being a woman and the first in my entire family (both immediate and extended) to attend a university in general, particularly one in the United States, is an incredibly humbling accomplishment. However, these same circumstances made my college experience exhausting, and there were definitely times I did not think I would complete my degree.

My experience with mental health was nonexistent, because for most of my life I'd been ingrained with the notion that personal matters don't get discussed, especially outside the home. During the second semester of my freshman year, I took a peer mentor training course that was a prerequisite to interning in the First-Year Experience program at my university. This course helped me learn about myself and my identity in the university. Not only that, but the professor became one of the most influential people in my life, helping me succeed during my time in college and one who to this day remains a mentor.

Because of the feedback that the professor provided in our assignments and in class, and her availability to meet with students during office hours, I started to trust her as someone I could confide in. This was the first time I trusted someone enough to share the personal challenges that I had been facing since my arrival in California. Through the self-reflection activities in class and my conversations with the professor, I began to recognize my symptoms of depression. This completely changed the course of my college career.

Depression remains very taboo and ignored in my culture. When I told my college professor about my experiences, she encouraged me to see a counselor. My automatic response was no, but she offered to walk me to the office and shared her experience with mental health. She also told me how ignoring it could affect my success in college. At 18 years old I finally trusted an outsider with personal matters, and I was offered nothing but support and kindness.

Throughout my years in higher education, I have had professors who shared their stories of being a first-generation college student, of personal struggles that they went through, and of how they got into their respective fields. I am blessed because I have had professors like this one who helped me see myself differently and whose examples I now follow. Research on the impact of narratives shows that stories are a way to connect. These are so important in students' lives, because if just one student is motivated or sees a different future self that they didn't before, that is one more student who is supported. How many students have left school because they felt that no one saw them? Too many.

ↀ

Serving as Career Mentors

The value of professor–student relationships extends beyond the academic experience. Faculty can serve as career mentors, helping students discover career paths in various fields, giving students opportunities to gain experience and skills, and helping them develop or expand their professional network. Although most colleges and universities offer career counseling, students are more likely to get career information from faculty than from career counselors (Greenbank & Hepworth, 2008). This is likely because students are more comfortable seeking guidance from someone they know and trust. Because faculty and students spend approximately 45 hours together each semester, it's not surprising that they would turn to faculty for career advice and information.

There are many variables that can impact whether professors and students engage in career conversations. For example, professor–student relationships are, not surprisingly, more common in smaller versus larger classes. In an interesting study by Beattie and Thiele (2016), it was found that larger classes had a more negative impact on Black students as they were less likely to interact with their faculty about careers. Although this was not the case for Latinx students, Latinx students were less likely to engage in conversations with their peers about careers. Beattie and Thiele (2016) noted that "large classes might magnify preexisting racial marginalization in important ways that undermine opportunities to interact with professors and peers" (p. 354). Based on national survey data, McClenney (2007) noted that part-time students were also less likely to engage in career conversations with their professors than full-time students. To address these equity issues, faculty will want to intentionally reach out and engage students, especially students of color and part-time students, in conversations about careers.

Faculty serving as advisers play an important role in career exploration and decision-making. Students appreciate the opportunity to reflect on their values, interests, and abilities with a faculty member they trust. Having the opportunity to discuss career paths with someone in the field can help students determine if they are on the right path. In the following student story, Sarah explains how her preceptor validated her career path and increased her motivation and engagement.

Advising Days
Sarah Harvey
*First-year student | Political Science | Stockton University
Course: Advising and Preceptors (small, in-person class)*

Precepting or advising days are very stressful as a student, and having a preceptor who can make you feel at ease and guide you on the right path is important. My preceptor does a great job of starting out our meetings in a casual way by asking me about my semester and other classes and how I am feeling. I find this help-ful and engaging because it shows she cares about my well-being and that I am not just another appointment to get through during the day. I appreciate that she leaves plenty of time for us during the meeting to be able to talk in-depth about my current plan and other future opportunities.

She helped me realize that my major is the right choice for me. When we discussed my educational plan, she encouraged me to take challenging courses in the field. Her encouragement and faith in me to take courses I would not neces-sarily have thought I was ready for gave me confidence in my skills and solidified in my mind that I was meant for this major. She also helped me find opportunities outside of the classroom for me to expand my knowledge in my field, whether it be an internship, the political science honor society, or research opportunities. When I know that there are interesting opportunities in my field of study, then I am more motivated to stay engaged and present in my current courses and take my future course planning more seriously. Through these experiences and my conversations with my preceptor, I am confident that I should be a political scientist.

Because I have a personal connection with my preceptor and know that she is invested in my education and well-being, I trust her to guide me when it comes to choosing classes and determining which opportunities to further investigate. From my point of view, I see precepting as a way for me and my adviser to connect and use our time to form an achievable plan for my academic success, as well as suc-cess after graduation. The basics of being a successful preceptor, in my opinion, are leaving enough time to have a productive conversation, making the student feel valued, being supportive, and sharing opportunities and ideas with the student.

෨෨

One of the best ways that students can explore, discover, and validate career interests is through experiential learning opportunities. Faculty can inform students of learning opportunities in their field so that they can gain valuable experience while also finding out more about their major and career options. In the following example, David shares how one of his professors invited him to participate in a lab and how this experience helped him see the many career possibilities in his field of interest. He reports that this was an incredibly valuable experience.

Invitation to Work in a Lab
David Lont
Junior | Aerospace Engineering | Western Michigan University
Course: Statics (small, in-person class)

Most undergraduate students majoring in STEM [science, technology, engineering, and mathematics] will have to complete at least some coursework in a lab—whether for physics, chemistry, or some natural science class—but most undergraduates will not be given the opportunity by their professors to work in the lab independently of their class. Of course, it might not be feasible to permit everyone in a class to work in a lab due to constraints in time, funds, or class size, but this experience is very beneficial, especially for students who are interested in undergraduate research or science. I know firsthand the impact this can have because I myself was given this opportunity to work in a lab when I completed my sophomore year in college.

I had stepped into my statics professor's office the last day of finals week in the fall to pick up one of my previous graded exams. I was expecting a quick visit when instead he invited me to sit down and chat for a few minutes. Apparently, he wanted to get to know me better after being in his class for a semester. It wasn't long before my professor mentioned his research where he worked alongside an aerodynamics professor in the fluid mechanics lab. He was very friendly and promised me he'd show me around the lab the following semester.

When I saw him again that following semester, he asked me if I would like to get involved with one of their graduate students who could use my help on a project if I was interested. I happily accepted and volunteered a couple of hours every week. When the spring semester ended, I had the opportunity to apply for a state grant through my university to do research that summer. I was awarded the grant and worked as a research assistant in the fluid mechanics lab alongside two PhD students working with particle image velocimetry, a technique used to visualize fluid flows.

Working in the lab taught me the importance of mastering the material from each class I had been taking for my major. I came to see how the knowledge I had gained through these classes translates to the practical world. I would have not had this engaging experience, however, had it not been for this professor showing an interest in me and inviting me to work in the lab. This experience opened my eyes to look at the bigger picture in engineering. This firsthand experience inspired and encouraged me to excel in my classes but also excited me even more about the sciences of fluids and aerodynamics. This experience helped me see various career paths in my field.

Providing a student with the unique opportunity to work in the lab independently of the student's class is an empowering way for professors to help students more deeply engage with their field of study. However, this cannot happen without a cherished professor–student relationship. Therefore, I encourage all professors to display trust and interest in their students and to engage more students with the opportunity to work in a lab environment, which will stimulate their interest in their field and ultimately prepare them for success. Professors have the power to positively impact their student's career paths if they are willing to open doors for their students.

ळ৵ঠ

Sometimes conversations and experiences help students determine that their initial career path is not what they expected. When this happens, students can explore other options. There is value, especially when this happens at the beginning versus the end of a college journey, in finding out there are other career options or paths that better align to interests and values. In the following example, Serena discusses how professor–student relationships helped her discover her passion and how this resulted in her changing her career path.

Changing Career Paths
Serena Rose Arandia
Junior | English | California State University, Stanislaus
Courses: Principles of Physiology and Creative Writing
(midsized, in-person classes)

I was previously attending Merced Junior College as a nursing major. I was fully committed to doing the work, but I was not fully committed to the profession. Professor Cary Coburn saw that and addressed it. I came in one day to talk to him about the grade I had in his class. I wasn't failing, but I was darn close to it. He sat me down and asked me if this is really what I wanted to do.

He saw my potential in writing and asked me to consider a different major. He saw my strengths and pushed me toward a different path. That same semester, I was in a creative writing class that was just for fun. I was encouraged to write stories, plays, poems, and all that jazz, and it all felt so natural. My professors were encouraging from the start, but when I told them about my possible change in major, I was pleased to see big smiles on their faces. I was inspired by their stories and the stories of guest speakers who helped me see that it's okay to change paths. My confidence in my writing was underdeveloped, but their positive encouragement and constructive criticism, both on paper and in person, nurtured my love for English and my writing skills.

Having a good relationship with my professors helped me change my career path. When Professor Coburn saw that my drive and my talent genuinely belonged elsewhere, he was comfortable enough to tell me, and I trusted him enough to listen to his suggestion. My professors were inviting, creative, and overall amazing people and professors. Because of their mentorship, doors for future jobs and successes have opened for me. They changed my life, and as I start off fresh at California State University, Stanislaus, I am excited about pursuing a career path that I know for a fact is for me.

❧

Helping Students Build a Professional Network

In addition to helping students discover and explore career options through conversations and experiences, faculty can also assist students with making professional connections. Networking is important, and the sooner students start to develop their professional network the better (Vilorio, 2011). Those with larger and stronger networks are more likely to be employed (Van Hoye et al., 2009). Growing a professional network is particularly important for students who enter college with less social capital and lower-status networks. In an interesting study by McGuire (2000), it was found that women and people of color are less likely to have high-status networks but that once they were given "the opportunity to interact with high-status employees, they were just as likely as White men to have high-status network members" in their networks (p. 517). As one would expect, having access to higher-status members in a network opens doors to more advanced and financially rewarding opportunities. Faculty can help combat inequities by helping students who walk into college with more limited access to high-status members develop professional networks that include high-status members.

Networking is an overwhelming, challenging task for many students. One way to support student skill development and confidence with networking is to assign tasks where students will need to interact with professionals in the field. Providing high levels of support and guidance through examples and models can ensure that students are prepared for assignments that require networking. One very effective assignment that helps students build a professional network while also learning about their career field is the informational interview. In an informational interview, students ask a professional who works in the field they are interested in questions about their career and the field and advice for those interested in the field (Crosby, 2010). Face-to-face and virtual job shadowing have been found to be effective ways to help students learn about career options (Padron et al., 2017). In the following student story, Jaclyn shares how helpful it was to conduct an informational interview with professionals in the hospitality field. This experience helped her better understand the expectations of the field in addition to building her professional network.

Interviewing Industry Professionals
Jaclyn Bonacorda
Senior / Event Management and Hospitality Management
University of Central Florida
Course: Strategic Leadership and Management (midsized, hybrid class)

The Rosen College and the Central Florida Hotel and Lodging Association host networking events each week to allow students to connect with industry professionals. Professor Lavendol required us to attend one of these sessions and interview an industry professional about the current state of the industry and seek advice for soon-to-be graduates. The purpose of the assignment was to strengthen our networking and interviewing techniques, to gain insight from industry leaders, and to learn more about what it means to be a leader in the hospitality industry.

Interviewing a hospitality leader from a top company helped me better understand the industry through the eyes of someone who has worked in hospitality almost her entire career. It also helped with building my professional network and expanding my career opportunities, as the person I interviewed asked if I would be interested in working for her company postgraduation. Although networking can be overwhelming, this assignment helped me to gain more experience talking with senior management, a task required on a regular basis in hospitality.

It also increased my knowledge of the industry. Reading textbooks and news articles about the hospitality industry provides some information, but it is even better to hear the real-life experiences of someone who has made their career working in hospitality. Another engaging aspect of the assignment was presenting what we learned from our interview to the rest of the class. Hearing all my classmates' different experiences with the leaders they interviewed kept me engaged, because I was genuinely interested in the advice they were given and learned a lot about various companies in the industry.

No matter what our major and what industry we find a career in, networking with industry professionals is something we will all need to do. I would encourage professors to find a way to motivate their students to start practicing this skill while still in college. It helps students build a valuable skill set and make connections to the professional community outside of the classroom.

❧

Faculty can also use their professional networks to encourage student growth and assist students with discovering opportunities. As experts in the field, faculty know many professionals who may be able to mentor or assist students as they pursue their career interests. Making connections for students, especially students who may have limited or lower-level status networks, can be of significant value to students. Faculty will be more inclined to make connections and recommendations to students when they have a relationship with the student outside of the classroom. In the following example, Rosalyn talks about how a professor she met through an extracurricular activity helped her make professional connections that assisted her with a project and led to a research position.

Networking Connections
Rosalyn Stoa
*Senior / Psychology and Business Administration /
University of Wisconsin, Green Bay*
Course: Extracurricular activity (small, in-person class)

I spontaneously signed up for our campu's Innovation in Aging competition and was placed in a random group consisting of an entrepreneurial business major; an engineer; and me, a psychology major. We created a sleek cup that was designed to counteract tremors for individuals with Parkinson's disease. This already exists in a sippy cup format, but we wanted to create something that would not demean the user. After winning this competition, we were in the running for the state-level Big Idea Tournament—something none of us expected to participate in.

Professor Ryan Kauth, the entrepreneurial guru on campus, became our mentor. We met with him, and he connected us to everyone we needed in the community. We were linked with a manufacturer and several innovative start-up companies. We were also referred to other professors on campus who could help us with the project. We met with these professionals to understand how an idea becomes a prototype, a product, and a customer solution. Professor Kauth also set up a practice pitch session for us with local innovators so that they could critique our lean start-up plan.

We didn't end up winning that competition, but it was a useful experience nonetheless. The process challenged me, from product conception to business design to networking. Professor Kauth's connections helped us develop a strong business model and product. He continued to reach out to us after the competition was over, pushing us to create a patent for it and sending us all the business competitions that came his way in case we wanted to participate. He still reaches out to me occasionally about the goings-on in my life and informed me about an interesting research position. He also introduced me to the keynote speaker at a business banquet we both happened to be attending. His connections have been incredibly useful, especially from an interdisciplinary standpoint.

For faculty: You have great networks. Use them, and help your students use them. Share your contacts if the interest fits. Pass on the emails you get about jobs, competitions, graduate school, events, and other things that your students might be interested in. It might just push them out of their comfort bubble. It will help them know you care. Sometimes students just need a little push to engage in learning outside of the classroom.

⚮

Although most think about building a professional network with those already working in the field, it is important for students to also see the value of peers. Classmates will soon become colleagues. Thus, building strong relationships with peers is an excellent way to help students develop a professional network that can serve as a source of support in college and has the potential to open doors after graduation. In the following example, Danielle, a first-generation graduate student, shares how her adviser created a professional network among full- and part-time advisees. Assisting part-time students with developing these strong relationships with peers is particularly important because part-time students often report not being as connected as their full-time student counterparts (McClenney, 2007).

Creating a Professional Network Among Advisees
Danielle V. Lewis
First-generation graduate student who is a working professional and mother
Higher Education | University at Buffalo

My PhD adviser is incredibly intentional in building a community of support in her advisee cohort. When a peer is accepted into our doctoral program, Professor Sallee sends a note to the entire group, welcoming the new addition to "Team Sallee." She then coordinates a social outing so that we can begin building relationships with the latest member of our team. These social outings occur regularly and are scheduled on days that all can attend. The venue and activity are jointly selected by members of the group. Activities have included bowling, an escape room, and shared meals. She also helps us coordinate writing groups that meet biweekly, coaches us in writing proposals for academic conferences in a group setting, and shares news of team members' celebrations electronically, encouraging us to publicly support one another.

By facilitating relationships among her advisees, this faculty member creates an environment in which students further along in the doctoral program offer feedback and mentorship to those newer to graduate studies. It is important to note that creating a team like this is perhaps more difficult at our institution than others, as this PhD program is composed of both full-time students and those who work full time and are enrolled part time. The graduate experience can vary immensely for students with these two enrollment statuses, yet this group of advisees is highly team oriented and works diligently to enhance their relationships with one another.

Professor Sallee's team approach to building relationships among advisees has resulted in supportive relationships that celebrate and support one another's successes. Students present their papers in advance of academic conferences and share dissertation proposals before defending to committees or to their team. This results in us being better scholars and producing higher-quality academic work.

Faculty who have considered facilitating a team environment for advisees should be encouraged by Professor Sallee's example. If you are not sure where to start in building a team environment, ask your advisees! Taking the time to really consider how they want to create or enhance relationships with one another can be a worthwhile exercise. Professor Sallee's efforts have made a significant impact on the experience of those she advises, not only between herself and individuals but also among advisees themselves. Because of the environment that Professor Sallee has created, the advisees who hope to become faculty members themselves will likely support one another after graduation and also replicate the experience she has provided, perpetuating a culture of both challenge and support among doctoral students, which certainly contributes to engagement and learning.

ॐ

Faculty Reflection Questions

1. What information can I share about myself to help students get to know me?
2. How can I use class activities or assignments to help me get to know my students?
3. How can I develop a professor–student relationship with students who are different from me?
4. How can I encourage students, especially those who may not typically do so, to visit with me outside of class?
5. What approaches can I use to connect with students who may be facing challenges?

6. How do I support students with their career decision-making and development?

7. What opportunities can I create and/or share with my students to help them achieve their goals?

8. How can I assist students, especially those with lower-status connections, with developing and enhancing their professional network?

3

TEACHING STRATEGIES

One of the best ways that faculty can engage students is by using effective and inclusive teaching strategies. What happens in the classroom plays a major role in student motivation, engagement, and learning. Delivery approaches such as storytelling, demonstrations, and interactive lectures have been found to be connected to high levels of student engagement (Tews et al., 2015). Findings from this same study, however, found that simply using fun activities, such as playing music and games, was not related to increased student engagement. Thus, it is not about entertaining students, but rather giving students meaningful opportunities to engage with the content and one another.

A variety of teaching methods can be used to engage students and increase their learning. Although many faculty have been encouraged to use new and innovative active learning approaches, tried and true teaching methods are also still valuable. Harrington and Zakrajsek (2017) provide evidence that the lecture is an effective teaching method, especially when active learning opportunities are used to help students understand the big ideas of the lecture. During lectures, faculty can demonstrate concepts or processes and provide students with opportunities to discuss and reflect on what is being learned. In a research study conducted by Griffin and Howard (2017), students had the highest levels of student engagement when this interactive lecture approach was used even when compared to other evidence-based teaching strategies. Gubera and Aruguete (2013) also suggested incorporating collaborative activities into lectures rather than replacing the lecture with collaborative learning tasks, because students performed better when lecturing was a part of the learning experience.

One of the reasons that lectures can work so well is that faculty will often skillfully weave stories into their lectures. Stories and personal examples get students emotionally engaged. When students are emotionally engaged, they will devote more cognitive resources to the task at hand, which enables them to be focused on learning and be less distracted by other stimuli such as their phones (Cavanagh, 2019).

Students also exhibit high levels of engagement when faculty use collaborative learning activities. Millis (2014) notes that collaborative learning has many benefits for students, including fostering deeper levels of learning. A variety of collaborative learning tasks such as partner work or small group discussions or projects can be used to increase student engagement and learning. Although it can be more of a challenge to incorporate opportunities for collaborative learning in large classes, it is advantageous to do so. Durham et al. (2018) found that modifying the curriculum for students in a large lecture so that it included opportunities for small group discussions positively affected student engagement.

Making It Personal

Making lessons personally meaningful can result in higher engagement and achievement. In a study exploring what worked best for minority students in terms of teaching and learning, Mushi (2001) found that students appreciated it when professors related their experiences to the content. Student interest is piqued when they see a real-world connection to the content, especially when it has immediate value to them. The better the faculty know their students, the easier it will be for them to use examples that have immediate personal relevance. In a study conducted by Muddiman and Frymier (2009), students identified several ways that faculty help them see the relevance of a course. For example, students reported that making connections to their current and future lives, sharing personal stories, and identifying real-world examples were helpful.

According to expectancy-value theory, students are more likely to be motivated when they expect to be successful with the task at hand and when they perceive the task to be of high value (Eccles & Wigfield, 2002). Faculty can help students in both regards: providing support and guidance to increase the likelihood of perceived success and explicitly communicating the value of the course and related tasks. To help students see the value of a task, faculty can share personal examples and help students make connections between the content and their personal lives. When faculty share personal experiences and stories, the content comes alive. Espino-Bravo (2015) notes that sharing personal stories that relate to the course content can prompt students to do the same.

In the following student story, Joshua, a first-generation student, shares how the professor's stories helped him get and stay engaged in the course.

Sharing Personal Experiences

Joshua Allen Brown
First-generation senior who is employed full time / Sociology
Kennesaw State University
Course: Foundations of Social Theory (small, in-person class)

One of the more memorable courses I have had stands out because of the multitude of personal narratives and experiences the professor embedded in his lectures. Rather than being a verbal overview of the chapters, the lectures were designed so well that the textbook material was supplemented and enriched through the examples shared by my professor. As someone who tends to become bored easily in the classroom setting, it was unusual for me to not want to miss a class. Because the professor integrated his own examples into the lessons, I found the class to be incredibly stimulating and enjoyable.

If I had read the assigned related readings for the course that day, the lecture successfully clarified the theories by offering more historically relatable, modern experiences through which my professor had actually lived. This helped me understand concepts that were difficult to grasp because the examples made it immediately relevant and placed the information in a more understandable context. And if I had happened to not have read the material beforehand, when I got around to doing so, it was subsequently easier to take in. Either way, this made me recall the information far more easily, and even now I continue to find myself using examples from his life experiences as memorable ways to recall sociological concepts.

The engagement did not come from only the content of the personal stories but also the way he delivered the stories. He was excited, engaging, and genuinely enthusiastic about the topic. His passion was contagious, increasing my own enthusiasm for learning. He also used examples from personal experiences that we may have had as students.

While covering a rather large amount of content, we moved through it quickly and effectively. There were no visual aids outside the occasional writing on the whiteboard, but I doubt even a well-designed digital aid would have done much if anything to engage me compared to his stories. As much as I enjoy and am accustomed to having technology as a tool for learning, I never felt that its absence in his class was to my detriment. Both knowing that I would learn something new and anticipating that I would enjoy doing so engaged me to be present physically and mentally.

ॐ

Research shows that student motivation is higher when students see the relevance of the examples being used in class. In a study conducted by Finney and Pyke (2008), students responded favorably and with high levels of motivation when local case studies featuring alumni were used. When professors personalize the learning experience to student interests and examples they can relate to, students will likely be interested in learning and perceive the value of the content or task.

These connections can facilitate learning because new concepts are linked to already existing knowledge (Priniski et al., 2018). Students appreciate it when faculty make connections between the content and what they already know (Rodriguez & Koubek, 2019). Connecting course content to student interests was the strategy most identified by students as a way to help them see the relevance of the course in a study conducted by Muddiman and Frymier (2009). These findings nicely illustrate that motivation and learning are improved when students focus on the relevance and real-world applications of the content. It also makes for a much more personalized learning experience.

In the following example, Laura shares how her professor used an assignment at the beginning of the semester to discover what students were passionate about and then integrated examples aligned with student interests into the course.

A Tailored Learning Experience
Laura Goldfarb
Senior / Communication Studies and Political Science / Wilfrid Laurier University
Course: Writing for Politics and Policy (midsized, in-person class)

As I reflect on my third year of study, one course—Writing for Politics and Policy—stands out from the rest as exceptionally engaging. Unlike most classes, which inevitably see declining attendance rates as the semester goes on, this course had almost every student coming back week after week. Professor Andrew Monti shattered the "one-size-fits-all" model of curriculum building. Instead of trying to make students interested in a predetermined set of topics, he inquired about the interests of each student and tailored his lectures according to what we were already curious about.

He set this technique in motion during the first class when he told us to write a two-page essay on a political issue—*any* political issue. We were given a few guidelines and almost no restrictions; our only instruction: Write about something that truly fascinates you. After the professor had read all the papers, he came to class with a slideshow presentation showing the distribution of our interests. Eleven people were interested in environment/energy issues, 10 in media, eight in education, and so on. He talked through each topic, expressing his own thoughts and sharing sources, always speaking directly to those students who expressed interest in the subject.

The course then proceeded as Professor Monti had planned. For a few weeks, we learned about the evolution and significance of language and media. Then, more specifically, core issues in politics and political language. And in the last third of the course, we analyzed propaganda, select campaigns, and an array of policies. But instead of including arbitrary examples along the way, Professor Monti animated each topic with examples relating to our expressed interests. For example, instead of explaining the concept of propaganda by using the most widely recognized examples of it, which is so often done in university classrooms, he chose a variety of lesser-known examples, but ones that he knew would speak directly to a group of us. I knew that every time I went to that class I would learn about people, events, and theories that genuinely intrigued me, and that is what kept me engaged throughout the entire semester.

Then, for our major assignment—a group project to create a communication campaign in support of a specific policy—he put up the original slideshow presentation with our interest distributions and created our groups from those lists. That meant that everyone would collaborate with classmates with whom they shared an interest. I did not know the other members of my group, but we quickly found ourselves in rapt conversation. We truly cared about the project that we were creating together, and because of that, we put far more effort into it than we would have if the groups and topics were randomized.

All in all, Professor Monti created a learning environment in which no student felt anonymous. Before he taught us anything, he gave us an opportunity to teach him about ourselves, and then he made the effort to relate to each of us through our academic interests. After witnessing Professor Monti's success, my advice to professors who want to capture the attention of their students is to learn about what your students are already interested in, whether that is done by assigning a short essay at the beginning of the semester, facilitating an in-class activity or discussion, or simply asking your students to write you an email. You will be able to not only better curate the more flexible parts of your curriculum but also make each individual student feel seen.

☙❧

As faculty consider the personal examples they share and encourage students to do the same, it is important for these stories and examples to resonate with all students, especially those from underrepresented groups.

> It is particularly important to make sure that all of your students feel equally welcome and equally valued in the conversation. Students whose identities and backgrounds vary from those of the rest of the class (in terms of gender identity, race, ethnicity, nationality, disability status, social class, etc.) may feel less able to easily join the community, and so it is critical that you plan carefully how to help them feel included. (Cavanagh, 2019, Principle 03 section, para. 3)

Intentionally using inclusive language and examples that represent various cultures will increase the likelihood that all students will feel a sense of belonging and be engaged.

Faculty will also want to think about various ways that students can feel invited to conversations. Not every student will feel comfortable expressing their thoughts or sharing their experiences in a large group discussion but may be comfortable doing so in small groups, in an anonymous online discussion, or perhaps through written assignments.

In the following student story, Benjamin shares how a note card assignment provided him with a way to reflect on and share an anti-Semitic experience he had and the value of that reflecting and sharing.

A Note Card Activity
Benjamin Sackler
Senior | Political Science | College of Charleston
Course: Religion in American Politics (small, in-person class)

It is not always easy to participate in class. Every student has valuable ideas or input, but not everyone is comfortable participating in class discussions. Fear may stop students from contributing their ideas, or students who are comfortable sharing their thoughts may not be called on by the professor before the discussion shifts or class ends. It's not always a given that students can share what they are thinking. This is why the note card assignment that my professor used was so effective.

This assignment, which was introduced on the very first day of class, was an ongoing assignment, lasting the entire semester. The task was simple: Every student was to hand in 15 note cards by the end of the semester (maximum of two per week) reflecting either material discussed in class or something outside of class that related to the material discussed in class. The actual writing assignment was broad; students were able to write objective accounts of situations or subjective, personal reactions to the material of their choosing. If this was accomplished, we got full credit for the assignment—no judgment, no bias, just honest, pure reflection.

This assignment helped me more than I could have imagined. At the beginning of the semester, I assumed this ongoing assignment would be more of a nuisance than anything. However, it took only a week before I realized the value of the assignment. During a night out in Charleston, South Carolina, I experienced a subtly anti-Semitic experience. It was nothing major, but I was hurt. I felt uncomfortable and uneasy. In the class prior to this experience we discussed a resurgence of anti-Semitism in America, in light of the recent Pittsburgh shooting. As a Jew, I had not experienced much anti-Semitism in my life. Sure, there was the occasional insensitive comment here and there, but nothing significant. However, after the shooting and the experience at the bar, a sense of fear filled me. Am I a potential target? Should I be hesitant to tell people about my heritage? I didn't know what to do with these thoughts until I realized this was a perfect opportunity to write them down on a note card.

My professor was appreciative of my input, which was validating. However, it was the assignment that I was especially thankful for. This experience is something I would not have been comfortable bringing up in class. Without the note card assignment, I quite possibly would not have had an outlet for these feelings. Writing my feelings about this experience was not only comforting but also allowed me to have an educational experience and to synthesize the material from the prior class lesson.

This assignment should be implemented by professors who teach both discussion-based and lecture-style classes. In a discussion-based class like mine, this assignment allows those who are shy in an in-class setting to get their point across to their professor. Discussion-based classes can be extremely intimidating for more reserved students, making this assignment helpful. Although I am an active participant in class, there are still things I am not comfortable speaking about in the class, and there isn't always an opportunity for me to share my thoughts, making this assignment useful for all types of students. In lecture-style classes, this assignment allows professors to hear from their students, which is a rarity in a lecture-style class. Even if there isn't time during class to hear from students, the note card assignment can allow students to have their voices heard.

❧

Helping students discover their own personal connections to the course content can also substantially increase student motivation. This was illustrated in a double-blind experimental study conducted by Hulleman et al. (2017). In this study that focused on highlighting the relevance of the course, students assigned to experimental conditions were asked to write about how the course material related to their life while students in the control group were asked to summarize what they had learned so far. Results indicated that students in the experimental groups who wrote about the relevance of the material to their own lives performed better on the final exam and were more interested in the subject matter compared to the students in the control group who instead summarized content. This intervention had the greatest impact on low-performing male students. This research shows that students benefit from the opportunity to make connections between the course content and their current and future lives.

Teaching strategies focused on careers can engage students. Although students will gain value from learning experiences that center around their interests, some students may not have clearly defined interests. College is a time where many students discover interests and areas of passion. Not every student will walk into college with a clear passion. Through college experiences, students will likely be introduced to new concepts and ideas, and as a result this can give rise to new interests and passions. Some students may need support with discovering what they are passionate about. Although student services such as career centers can provide assistance, faculty can also play an important role in this process. In the following example, Genevieve describes how strategies in a personalized course focused on career helped her determine her interests and passion in her very first semester.

Discovering Your Passion
Genevieve Jaser
Junior who is employed part time / Interdisciplinary Studies with concentrations in English and Communication / Southern Connecticut State University
Course: Intellectual/Creative Inquiry (small, in-person class)

In Intellectual/Creative Inquiry class, the first class of my first year, I walked in uncertain about what would be taught and not sure what benefit this course would have for me. Professors Katie De Oliveira and Crystal Cyr had an active and engaging presence in class. There was a heavy focus on individuality and finding and pursuing your passion, which connected to the first-year research experience project. Creative freedom was encouraged, and both professors consistently met on a one-to-one basis with students to sculpt the most approachable and researchable idea for each student. The personalized aspect of the class allowed me to focus deeply on what was important to me while benefitting from the support system that my professors provided.

For first-year students, the idea of being "set free" to find what they love is daunting, but when backed by a support system of professors and staff members who encourage and guide the individual, this approach becomes a great opportunity for self-expression and growth. This can be achieved by allowing students to engage in conversations without too much intervention. To help a confused, discouraged, or uninterested individual, it is helpful to ask what they are interested in, what they hope to do in the world, what they love. One can't force someone to want to do something, but every student has passion, whether they know it or not, and, once found, the student will become more engaged with the course.

During the one-on-one meetings, my professors listened. When a professor takes time to ask me questions, I become much more open and receptive to feedback in the future. My professors encouraged me to question what I loved and to develop my passions through an academic assignment. For the first-year research experience project, I became increasingly interested in the idea of leadership. When my ideas developed throughout different stages of the project, my professors encouraged me and helped me find my voice.

The personal connections with my professors also helped me beyond the class. Once the class ended, I was offered the opportunity by my professors and the coordinators of the course to tutor others. From there, I connected with members of the Academic Success Center on campus and expanded my tutoring abilities to reach other class subjects.

ꙮ

Using Demonstrations

Demonstrations are an excellent way to help students see the value and relevance of learning tasks. Research has shown that instructor demonstrations are associated with higher levels of student engagement (Milne & Otieno, 2007; Tews et al., 2015). Demonstrations are shared learning experiences that can often evoke an emotional reaction. As a result, students are more likely to engage in conversations about the demonstration outside of class (Milne & Otieno, 2007).

Students are also more likely to remember content when their professors show and illustrate versus explain. A quasi-experimental study of 480 high school students revealed higher achievement scores for students who participated in a class where the teacher used demonstrations as compared to students in a class where lecturing without demonstrations was the teaching method used (Daluba, 2013). Evidence for the connections between demonstrations and improved achievement also comes from studies conducted at the college level. For example, Kim (2015) studied the effectiveness of using demonstrations in a statics undergraduate course. Results indicated that 94% of the first-year college students in this study were engaged in learning and that achievement scores, especially for low-motivated students, improved with this teaching method.

In the following student story, David shares how in-class demonstrations and a professor seeking feedback were especially helpful to him.

Interactive Demonstration in Physics
David Lont
Junior | Aerospace Engineering | Western Michigan University
Course: University Physics I (midsized, in-person class)

Sir Isaac Newton is one of my favorite historical scientists. He is well known for discovering the three laws of motion and for his works in calculus. When we are first introduced to his laws of motion, however, it is often difficult to grasp the implications of these concepts and formulas without the ability to see or understand what they represent. Thus, these concepts become mere symbols in formulas, which the student blindly learns to use to solve homework problems. To help students gain a clear picture in their mind of what Newton's several concepts entail, faculty can use an interactive demonstration in the classroom.

One of the most memorable interactive demonstrations I experienced was in University Physics when we were learning about the concept of force and what a newton is. I remember our professor went into the preparation room in the physics lecture hall and came back with a cart loaded with boxes filled with toy apples, each with a mass equivalent to the force of one newton on earth. She then explained that she wanted her entire class to experience the force of one newton in our hands and began tossing the toy apples at the entire classroom. I remember this was both exciting and fun for the entire classroom. I remember that when I got a chance to hold one of these toy apples in my hand, the concept of a newton as a force made more sense to me. I had previously learned about the newton in high school and understood that on earth its weight was about one-tenth of a kilogram, but this class activity allowed me to experience myself what the force of one newton was like on my hands.

Although this physics class was challenging, particularly during exams, I learned a lot from my professor because of her effective teaching strategies. Because my professor helped me understand Newtonian mechanics both conceptually and mathematically, later, when I went on to more advanced classes like statics and dynamics, I was able to quickly grasp the concepts introduced in these classes and to do well in them. Her lectures were complemented by several in-class activities such as solving problems in teams, clicker questions that provoked thinking on a given problem, and physics demonstrations that connected the theoretical world to the real world. Another thing I particularly admired about her was that she continuously asked for and welcomed student feedback from lectures, exams, quizzes, and homework through surveys and often had us send her our physics questions, which she then addressed in class the following lecture. I felt like my opinion and participation mattered in her class.

Interactive demonstrations in the classroom will make lectures more engaging and will also offer students a direct connection between the real world and the theoretical world being discussed in that class. Clearly illustrating how that topic connects to everyday examples enables students to engage mentally in class. I also would like to encourage more professors to welcome continuous student feedback, because it serves as a gauge of class comprehension and maintains constant student engagement. Such engaging classes can pave the road for a student's success in their future classes.

~~

In the next student story, Samantha also describes how examples and demonstrations helped her learn the course content. She explains that the examples used at the start of the class engaged her and how the demonstration helped her better understand the concepts being discussed. These teaching strategies enhanced her motivation and helped her retain information over time.

Examples and Demonstrations
Samantha Alger-Feser
Commuter graduate student | Psychology | University of Wisconsin, Green Bay
Course: Social Science Statistics (small, in-person class)

I have always hated math, which is why I was furious when my adviser told me I needed to take Social Science Statistics after I thought I was done with the subject for good. I walked into day one already wanting the class to be over for the semester, but Professor Kate Burns was so passionate about statistics that I soon grew to like it. In fact, I became her teaching assistant a year later because it was such a phenomenal class.

Most days Professor Burns would start class off with a statistics meme or joke. We would talk about it before starting class and then smoothly transition into the material for that day. For example, one day I walked into class and a photo of a doctor telling a male patient that he was pregnant, labeled Type I error, and a photo of a doctor telling an obviously pregnant female that she was not pregnant, labeled Type II error, was displayed on the screen in the front of the room. During one of our exams, I was struggling with a problem related to Type I and Type II errors. I visualized this picture in my head, and I got the correct answer. I thought it was great that Professor Burns opened her lecture with interesting examples because they really stuck with me.

Professor Burns also engaged students through demonstrations and interactive activities. For example, she brought in mini bags of M&Ms when we were learning about standard error. Each student counted how many blue M&Ms they had and then Professor Burns walked us through the formula. I found activities like this to be extremely helpful, and I still remember them. When teaching us about degrees of freedom, Professor Burns called four volunteers to the front of the room. She gave each student a choice of four highlighters (yellow, blue, pink, and green). When she got to the last student, she explained that he, unfortunately, had no choice in color and was therefore restricted to one option, the yellow highlighter. She then explained degrees of freedom in the context of statistics and the number of observations minus the number of restrictions. Now I will never forget the formula for degrees of freedom, and I did not even volunteer to participate. I remember wishing I did because I would have gotten a free highlighter! This teaching approach made the class enjoyable.

⚭

Research has shown that both live and online demonstrations can be valuable. For example, Sever et al. (2013) found that there was no difference between the academic performance of second-year college students studying education who watched live demonstrations versus those who watched a video demonstration. However, Rose (2018) found that online videos can be particularly advantageous in a large lecture class. Students in this study preferred watching a recorded video in class over live demonstrations because it was easier for them to see the demonstration when it was projected on a large screen. They also appreciated having the ability to rewatch it later as needed.

Online demonstrations are an excellent way to engage online learners. Although students taking online courses appreciate the flexibility and convenience of online courses, they often talk about how they miss the in-class experience. Online students are less likely to report having high levels of interaction and benefitting from faculty expertise compared to students taking face-to-face courses (Mather & Sarkans, 2018). The demonstration is one way that students can experience what Garrison et al. (2000) calls teacher presence. It is an excellent way for students to feel connected to the teacher and to also benefit from their expertise. Miller and Redman (2010) found that watching videos in an online class was educationally beneficial, as evidenced by higher exam scores. In the following example, Amy talks about her professor's use of video and synchronous learning opportunities in an online doctoral class and how these teaching strategies engaged her as a graduate student.

Videos and Synchronous Meetings in an Online Course
Amy Hankins
Graduate student who is a working professional | Community College Leadership
New Jersey City University
Course: Leadership Theory and Change Management (small, online class)

As a graduate student taking online classes toward a doctorate degree in educational leadership, I have found that my professors' use of video in our classes has aided in keeping my learning experience interesting and fresh. In my experience, both synchronous and asynchronous use of video can be excellent pedagogical tools in online learning. Here are some examples that come to mind regarding what has worked best to keep me engaged.

If an assignment has multiple components, an asynchronous video or screencast of a professor explaining the assignment step by step and showing examples can be incredibly helpful. For instance, one of my professors recently posted an instructional video she made while sitting in her home office. I watched her video once on my laptop, and then I watched it again later while I was on the treadmill to ensure I absorbed the instructions sufficiently. As graduate students, most of us have our phones or some sort of device with us constantly; we are on the go constantly, and so posted videos like this can be an excellent learning tool. One of my classmates listens to video postings on her way home from work to get her head wrapped around the intricacies of the assignments before she begins them.

I have also really enjoyed having synchronous online meetings. I live in the Midwest, and many of my fellow graduate students live out east, so to be able to meet face-to-face in real time is a huge boon for my learning experience. The nonverbal nuances that are lost via written correspondence are invaluable in getting to know someone on a deeper level. During these meetings, our professor works through examples, answers questions, and gives us an opportunity to work collaboratively with our fellow students. In addition to academic tasks, online meetings also gave us the opportunity to learn about each other's lives outside of academia. Personally, these meetings have helped me develop special connections, building friendships and trust. This example of online interaction was truly a powerful and meaningful experience.

Thankfully, my professor also scheduled meetings to check in with us individually. A one-on-one video conference was reassuring. Many of us have high expectations for ourselves regarding the quality of the work we produce, so getting face time with a professor or mentor to ensure we are on the right track is invaluable. My professor also set up webinars with national experts, giving us an opportunity to learn from and connect with leaders in the field. I come away from these meetings feeling contemplative, motivated, and often restored.

❧

Using Collaborative Activities

Another powerful way to engage students is through collaborative activities. When students work together on projects in and outside of class, they can develop strong connections with their peers. Group work can facilitate cross-cultural collaboration and assist students with developing interpersonal skills (Sweeney et al., 2008). Students who connect with their classmates are more likely to feel a sense of belonging, which often increases engagement levels.

Fostering a sense of belonging can be particularly important to students of color. In a study conducted by Case (2013), students of color were asked to identify exemplary faculty. Identified faculty were then interviewed about

the teaching approaches they used. Not surprisingly, many of the identified faculty members used cooperative learning methods and emphasized the
importance of understanding and responding to cultural dynamics in the
classroom. Working with a partner in class was also one of the strategies identified as useful by minority students in a study conducted by Mushi (2001).

Collaborative activities can also facilitate deeper levels of learning (Durham
et al., 2018; Sweeney et al, 2008). This was illustrated in a meta-analysis conducted by Swanson et al. (2019). Results of this study revealed that team-based
learning had a positive, moderate effect on students learning course content.

Unfortunately, many students report that they do not work with classmates on academic projects. According to national survey results, 68% of
community college students who completed the Survey of Entering Student
Engagement indicated that they never worked with a classmate on a project
outside of class, and 22% reported that they never worked with other students
on projects in class (Center for Community College Student Engagement,
2010).

Discussions

One of the simplest, yet still very effective, ways to engage students in collaborative work is through discussions. Roehling et al. (2011) conducted focus
groups with students in the millennial generation to understand whether
they found discussions valuable and if so why. The results of this study indicated that students did find discussions useful because they "(1) make learning more active, (2) result in a deeper understanding of the material, and (3)
promote perspective-taking" (p. 2). Discussions also enable students to get to
know one another and provide many opportunities for peer feedback.

In the following student story, Kayla, a graduate student, describes the
value of weekly student-driven discussions.

Student-Driven Discussions
Kayla Jasper
Graduate student | Social Work | Temple University
Courses: Clinical Practice With Individuals, Families, and Groups I and II
(small, in-person classes)

I entered my social work program with a group of students focusing on the same
career paths. My cohort became very close through classes and assignments that
required teamwork and collaboration. One especially engaging task was when we
were asked to openly share experiences with one another.

As part of my two-semester clinical courses, my professor gave us the opportunity to share questions, comments, and concerns with one another regarding
our practicum experiences. Each week, my clinical professor would tell us to take
out a piece of paper and write down anything we wanted to share with the class

about what was going on at our internship. On the paper, we rated each thought from one to three. Three meant we really want to talk about this issue, and one meant it could wait until next week to be discussed if time did not allow for it. For the most part, each issue brought up ethical dilemmas and situations that allowed us to offer different perspectives. A classmate could be struggling with a client situation, and the rest of us would provide feedback and help them consider different approaches to the situation.

By doing this, we were all able to work together and bring different ideas to the table. In my cohort, we all held different positions in various agencies and settings. We learned from one another and bounced ideas back and forth that forced each of us to think outside of the box. This kind of open collaboration and peer feedback through discussion strengthened our bond as a cohort while also expanding our clinical lenses.

The ongoing help and support that I received from professors, field administrators, and classmates helped me be successful. I believe it is extremely important for students to be able to look to others in the classroom as a support system, and professors and staff should aim to create a classroom that fosters this kind of environment.

❧

Many faculty regularly use discussions, but based on Kayla's story, student-led discussions are especially beneficial. This approach gives students ownership over their learning and as a result can increase both engagement and learning. As with other collaborative approaches, it can be helpful to provide a rationale and perhaps even some training on how to fully engage in and maximize the value of discussions. In an interesting study by Brank and Wylie (2013), students taking an advanced sociology course were required to participate in weekly discussions. At the start of the semester, students in the experimental condition participated in a discussion about why discussions were valuable and the role of discussions in learning while students in the control condition began weekly discussions without this initial conversation. The results of this study revealed that this prediscussion about discussions increased student engagement and learning. Specifically, students in the experimental group versus the control group had higher grades on a final paper, and they rated the course more positively. These results suggest that spending some time at the start of the semester on the why of the teaching approach can further enhance engagement and learning.

Faculty can also take on the role of facilitator during discussions to assist students with organizing ideas. Research has shown that collaborative opportunities that assist students with learning the content by using organizers increase motivation and academic performance. For example, in a study conducted by Goldberg and Ingram (2011), students who engaged in a variety of collaborative learning tasks, including developing concept maps and categorizing grids, found these to be valuable, indicating that these activities helped them see connections between concepts and understand the course material better.

In the following example, Claire, a first-generation community college student, explains how her professor used a small group thought organizer activity at the start of a large group discussion as a way to engage students.

Using Thought Organizers in Discussions
Claire Maloney
First-generation junior | International Business | Waubonsee Community College
Course: Humanities (small, in-person class)

In this class, the professor posed a question related to the content we would be discussing that day. He would write a word in a circle on the whiteboard. The question followed the structure of "What is . . . ?" For example, the professor introduced the topic of 3D art by asking, "What is space?" The student groups were tasked with answering the question in our own words. He would talk through the response with each group and make connections to other topics we've discussed. As the responses came in, the professor would diagram them out on the whiteboard, visually showing connections among concepts. At the end of this activity, he would provide a summary. During the rest of the class, he would frequently revisit the ideas provided in the thought organizer.

This was engaging for several reasons. Being able to brainstorm in a small group allowed for in-depth discussion. By establishing relationships with other students in the course, we became more comfortable sharing our ideas. Hearing the ideas of others and seeing all the ideas visually diagrammed made it easy to see the connections between concepts. It kept us motivated because we were responsible for contributing to the discussion and lesson.

This teaching technique probably works best in a setting where free interpretation of ideas is generally accepted. Faculty who want to try this teaching approach will want to anticipate responses so that these can be incorporated into the lesson plans. This thought organizer approach helped us see and discover the relationships between and among various concepts related to the course.

❧

Discussions in online classes can be especially important. When discussion prompts are crafted well to invite multiple perspectives, online discussions can engage students and assist them with mastering the course content (Aloni & Harrington, 2018). Online discussions that incorporate opportunities for peer feedback are rated as particularly engaging and useful by students (Cundell & Sheepy, 2018). The online discussion is often at the heart of an asynchronous virtual classroom, and it is therefore important to help students connect to one another and the content through meaningful conversations. In the following example, Sarah, a returning adult, online graduate student, shares her positive experiences with online discussions.

Online Discussions
Sarah Lyman Kravits
Returning adult, online graduate student, mother of three, who is employed
Education / Rutgers University, New Brunswick
Course: Introduction to Child Psychology (small, online class)

One of the central weekly tasks that Professor Golbeck incorporated into the work for this course was an online discussion page. Each week, she posted eight or nine questions related to that week's readings. The readings were to be completed over the course of the previous week so that students would have completed the reading by the first day that the related discussion questions were available for response. The questions became available on a Tuesday and were open for response until the following Monday at 11:59 pm.

Professor Golbeck was clear and detailed in how she described the response process in the syllabus, and she consistently reinforced the policy and the process each week. She required that students post at least nine responses to questions, with at least five being original responses to questions and four being responses to answers posted by other students. She required that students distribute their postings throughout the week, noting that a prime goal of this requirement was to encourage ongoing discussion among students all week long. When necessary, she would reinforce this policy, emphasizing that cramming all responses in on the last day or two of the week doesn't promote student interaction or allow for students to learn from one another.

In the syllabus and in announcements and communications with the students, Professor Golbeck requested that responses to questions were thoughtful, indicate an understanding of the readings, and show the application of central ideas. She was clear about welcoming a variety of ideas and perspectives and about the importance of separating people from specific positions. Over the course of the week, she regularly reinforced her expectations with follow-up responses that encouraged further discussion when students did not dig that deeply into a topic. She would also post new questions to spark more of an exchange.

The experience of posting to the discussion group throughout the week took my understanding of the readings and week's concepts to a much deeper level than if I had been working alone, and this is especially important in an online course when we are not sitting in a room together having a conversation. Because we were required to respond to others, we read one another's postings thoughtfully and, as a result, engaged in a meaningful exchange of ideas. We were exposed to different personal perspectives and experiences and benefited from the basic fact that different people focused on different parts of the readings. Many times I found myself reading an idea from another student that surprised or intrigued me, going back to the reading assignment to reread a section that the student had focused on, and finding myself with a new understanding—broader, perhaps, or more nuanced—than I would have come up with on my own.

For professors teaching an online course who want to promote collaborative engagement, my advice would be to build that collaboration into a weekly task with as much detailed instruction as possible. For a variety of reasons, many students will only do what is required of them and nothing more. The more specific you are about collaborative interaction—what to do, how often, in response to whom, and so on—the more students will collaborate meaningfully. The hope is that when students fulfill your requirements, they will find themselves engaged with their fellow students as I did, and thereby be motivated to go beyond the requirements and interact more and with greater depth.

❧

Group Projects

Faculty can also use group projects to engage students with one another and the course material. Caulfield and Persell (2006) report that when undergraduate students are assigned to research groups, they work harder and learn more. This was also found by Chiriac (2014) who reported that 97% of students who participated in semester-long groups indicated that the group experience facilitated their learning. Specifically, they reported learning more and different knowledge by participating in the group.

When students work together on long-term projects, they can get to know each other well and may even form long-lasting connections and relationships. Undergraduate and graduate students participating in semester-long group projects reported that this experience facilitated a sense of belonging (Chiriac, 2014). Trust in group members is key to successful outcomes, and trust develops over time. The importance of trust was illustrated in a study conducted by Ennen et al. (2015), who found a strong positive relationship between trusting group members and motivation and academic achievement. Instructors can help group members develop trust by giving students an opportunity to get to know one another, providing clear structures and expectations that emphasize interdependence, monitoring group member contributions, and intervening if the workload is not being evenly distributed.

Classmates can serve as a strong source of support and provide encouragement that can keep students engaged and motivated. Small groups can help students connect with their classmates, especially in large classes. The power of small groups is shared in the following student story. Sara discusses how being a part of a semester-long group helped her feel a sense of belonging, form friendships, and find her voice in discussions.

Semester-Long Group Work
Sara Idol
Junior / Nursing / Wichita State University
Course: Introduction to Sociology (midsized, in-person class)

In my Introduction to Sociology class, my professor—Jodie Simon—put all 75 students in groups determined by common interests. Interacting with our respective group members for the entire semester provided us with the opportunity to develop relationships with our peers and feel more comfortable speaking with other students and in front of a larger-sized class.

Professor Simon used a creative way to put us into groups. She had students write down five random statements about themselves. It could be anywhere from "I am an introvert" to "I love cats," or even "I love the show *The Office*." After completing this task, she had every single student get up and wander around the lecture hall to find people with similar interests, and they would sign their names under that specific statement. As soon as one statement reached five signatures, that student would proceed to the front of the classroom, and Professor Simon would enter them into a spreadsheet under their team name—which related to their shared interest. Once a group was assembled, those members could not be a part of another cohort, so the pool of students got smaller and smaller as the activity went on. Each group created an official team name, motto, team color, and a unique gesture to greet each other upon arrival into class, which was strange at first, but it was something that brought us all into more of a "team" rather than just a group.

This group approach allowed everyone in the class to branch out and meet people of diverse backgrounds and world views. Wichita State University has a high concentration of international students, so learning about the differences among perspectives from countries all over the world in a class like sociology really helps students take the learned information and apply it to the real world. Having a consistent group in class to discuss various topics during the lectures made talking to each other easier. Many of us became friends. This was especially helpful to me because I'm typically quite shy in classroom settings. In time, I felt more comfortable sharing my opinions with the whole class. These groups—along with the incredible professor—made the class more enjoyable. I know I was more motivated to show up and participate in class, even if it was an early morning class.

I highly encourage teachers and professors to categorize students in some way and to keep it consistent throughout the entire semester. This process fosters so many peer relationships. Many of us stayed in contact, forming study groups, attending school organizations together, or simply being friends. My biggest piece of advice for any faculty who wants to engage their students in their class, especially in discussions, is to create peer groups because they motivate students to participate and interact with the material presented.

☙❧

Group work is an opportunity for peers to support one another. Turner describes how his professor implemented a peer support model in the classroom where students helped one another learn the course content. This experience facilitated both a sense of belonging and an increased understanding of course content for Turner.

Peer-Supported Learning
Turner Smith
First-generation sophomore | Psychology | Kennesaw State University
Course: Introduction to Statistics (small, in-person class)

At the beginning of the statistics course, my professor told us that we would be helping each other throughout the course. I wasn't sure what this meant at first but soon discovered how helpful this teaching approach would be to me. After learning a new topic, the professor would give the class problem sets to practice individually. As students worked through the practice sets, the professor began to assess which students struggled and which students understood the coursework. The professor then partnered students who understood the material with those who seemed to be struggling. The small groups did not always consist of the same students. The small groups composed of approximately two to three students would then collaborate until everyone understood the material before moving onto something new or finishing the class. Simply put, this is a process of learn, practice, collaborate, repeat.

Personally, I was both a helper and the one who was being helped depending on the lesson. The experience of being able to hear how others logically process a problem opened my eyes to diverse ways of thinking that can lead to the correct answer. Working in a small group of up to three students helped me connect with fellow classmates and build a level of trust needed to make this style of learning effective.

This teaching method made me feel engaged and motivated to learn more. This helped the class in two important ways. First, it created a sense of belonging for all students because we had such close relationships with one another. It also helped me because this approach led to me having a deeper level of understanding of the content. When my classmates were explaining the topic from their perspective, it helped me learn. When I was the one helping, I loved watching other students experience a "light-bulb moment" when they finally understood the material they were initially confused about. We all genuinely wanted each other to excel, in and out of the classroom, which made an enjoyable experience for all students.

For faculty who want to use this approach, I suggest they explain the approach and the value of it in detail at the beginning of the semester. Allowing students to gain an understanding of a topic together will essentially help build the bond needed to foster a sense of belonging. All in all, I feel this is a great teaching method because it allowed the students to become involved during class time and we motivated and supported one another. I wish more professors with small class sizes would use this method.

తుళ

Collaboration is also critical in online courses. Unfortunately, collaborative activities beyond discussions are not always incorporated into online courses. Faculty teaching online courses are encouraged to structure online learning experiences that foster positive peer relationships through partner or group activities that align with the learning outcomes of the course. It is, however, important to understand the time constraints that online students may face. Students may be choosing online courses because they have inconsistent schedules that can make it challenging for them to find time to meet as a group. Although synchronous meetings can be advantageous, faculty can also provide asynchronous ways for students to collaborate on projects in online classes. Despite the challenges, online group work can increase motivation and learning.

In the following example, Edwin shares his positive experience with an online course that relied on teamwork.

Online Group Project
Edwin S. Lee
Graduate student / Library and Information Science / San Jose State University
Course: Information Professions (midsized, online class)

Recently, I was fortunate to take a class that gave me a chance to immerse myself in an online environment. In this class, the instructor assigned a group project that required students to research an organization. Before starting the project, the instructor asked students to share what type of career they wanted to pursue. Each student was then placed into a team based on their career interests. Students also had to complete modules to learn interpersonal skills that would be helpful for teamwork. After each team member completed the modules, each team was asked to elect a leader, assign roles to the remainder of the team members, and agree on rules for the project.

As each student worked on the project, they contributed to the research by performing their team duties and checking in with their teammates, as stated in their team rules. Along the way, the instructor helped by hosting online meetings and checking in with each team about their project progress. After students completed their group project, they presented it to the class as a team using videos.

The team-building learning strategy that the instructor used helped me engage with the course and form connections with other students. I enjoyed being placed in a group where other students and I had similar career goals. During weekly video conferences, we discussed the project and shared information about our professional and personal lives. Knowing my group members made me feel more comfortable asking questions when the material was unclear or I was confused.

I became eager to learn because my instructor provided information about career development while walking us through the class assignments. My instructor's tips about career development helped me understand why we completed specific assignments in the class. Furthermore, the instructor checking in with each group about the project progress seemed to help us stay focused and complete the tasks in a timely manner. This was a valuable experience, because I learned how to build an online team culture without ever meeting anyone on my team in person.

❧

Edwin's example highlights the importance of the faculty role in group projects. To facilitate these connections through groups and assist students with being productive, students benefit from faculty teaching them how to function effectively as group members. Students typically report receiving little to no training on how to engage in group work (Colbeck et al., 2000); however, research shows that training students leads to improved performance and outcomes (Sweeney et al, 2008). In an experimental study conducted by Prichard et al. (2006), students assigned to the training condition, which consisted of 90 minutes of training students on how to be productive in a group, outperformed students who did not receive this training. Training can be provided in person or online. In Edwin's example, each student had to complete an online training module prior to beginning the group project.

The instructor role goes beyond communicating the value of groups and sharing strategies on how students can engage in effective group work. Results of research conducted by Bailey et al. (2015) "suggest that instructor involvement and evaluation techniques provide both advocacy and structure that can facilitate proactive interpersonal processes within groups" (p. 182). Students recommend that faculty who assign groups provide oversight and clearly articulate the purpose of the group project at the start (Payne et al., 2006). Based on research conducted by Sarfo and Elen (2011), it is also very helpful to assign students individual work that relates to the group project. This way every student in the group is bringing ideas and resources to the conversation from the start.

After setting the stage for success, faculty will need to continue to support group members. Harris and Bristow (2016) suggest that faculty require students to complete weekly reflection logs that focus on group processes and group self-regulation to improve communication, experiences, processes, and the final product. This approach can help students monitor their progress and enable the instructor to stay up to date on how the group is functioning so that additional support can be provided as needed. When students perceive group work as valuable and find success in these experiences, they will undoubtedly have higher levels of engagement and achievement. In Edwin's story, the important role of the instructor throughout the semester was highlighted.

Collaborative learning experiences can extend beyond the classroom walls. Many professors incorporate out-of-class learning opportunities into their curriculum. These experiences help students connect to one another, the community, and the course content. Engaging students in group work that involves the community can be especially engaging.

This was the case in the student story that follows. Rosemary shares how her professor infused community-based learning into a course she was taking. This example shows how interactions outside of the classroom can be beneficial in terms of relationship building, engagement, and learning.

A Community-Based Learning Experience
Rosemary Brockett
Junior | Environmental Studies | Wilfrid Laurier University
Courses: Responding to the Syrian Refugee Crisis and
Syrian Refugee Integration in Canada (small, in-person classes)

In the first course, Responding to the Syrian Refugee Crisis, we studied the Syrian refugee crisis as it was occurring and being reported in the media. We discussed firsthand stories and media reports; debated the meaning of *refugee*; and heard from frontline responders to this crisis, such as refugee welcome centers, resettlement workers, social workers, and doctors. These were great learning experiences, but the best part of the course was the small group work we did in the community. In small groups, we got to know Syrian newcomer families by arranging for and cooking five meals together. We spent time throughout the semester at a local community kitchen, making hundreds of kebeh and many bowls of tabbouleh.

In the follow-up course, Syrian Refugee Integration in Canada, Professor Brockett had a similar design of active learning inside and outside the classroom, combining discussions and hearing from local organizations working with Syrian newcomers in the region. The small group work in this class involved partnering with Syrian newcomer families to organize events with them, which ranged from going to the Syrian families' homes to bowling, to cooking meals and playing games in a park.

These two courses taught by Professor Brockett were the most engaging courses I have taken in college. The courses were impactful, fun, challenging, and motivating like no other course due to the mixture of having discussions with my professor and peers, working through new situations with other students, and actually going out into the community and meeting the people being studied in class. I got to know my professor and became friends with other students. With the activities I did, the course felt fun and interactive, not like normal schoolwork. Furthermore, I came to understand the Syrian conflict and the challenges of integrating into a new culture in a profound, nuanced, and challenging way. Afraa, Rima, Mohammed, and Ghada, members of my Syrian family, helped me learn course material on a personal level.

I could not help but feel motivated and engaged in my schoolwork when taking these courses. All the elements of community and peer engagement caused me to look forward to class every week and to want to do the readings and assignments. I learned a huge amount through hearing the stories of the Syrians and speakers and being pushed outside of my comfort zone.

For professors seeking to engage students in collaborative learning experiences that extend into the community, I suggest you have students work together closely. Get them talking in small groups, put them in situations outside of their comfort zone, and give them tasks and responsibility. When you do these things, students will form bonds and friendships because they are forced to rely on each other. This, in turn, deepens learning. Sending students out into the community to work on projects is exciting, new, and challenging and provides motivation to work hard.

Faculty Reflection Questions

1. What culturally relevant examples can I share to make the lessons personally relevant to students?
2. How can I incorporate the interests of my students when I lecture?
3. What strategies can I use to help students make personal connections to the course content?
4. What live or virtual demonstrations can I use to help students become engaged and better understand the concepts being discussed?
5. How can I use videos and synchronous meetings in online courses to engage students and support their learning?
6. How can I best engage students in face-to-face and online discussions? How I can ensure that all students have a voice in the conversations?
7. What types of group projects can I use in my in-person and online courses to help students connect with one another while also diving deep into the course content?
8. How might I connect students to the community via group projects or other assignments?

4

MEANINGFUL ASSIGNMENTS

Well-crafted assignments are another way faculty can engage students. Assignments are one of the primary ways that students engage in the learning process outside of class. Assignments help students gain confidence and develop a higher sense of self-efficacy (Wollschleger, 2019). This is especially likely when assignments are used to challenge and stretch students. Terrenzini (2011) emphasized the important role of challenge in motivation. He noted that students exhibit higher levels of motivation when they are faced with different and challenging tasks. Assignments that are designed to push students outside of their comfort zone and foster high-level skills such as creativity and problem-solving can promote student engagement and learning, especially when faculty provide high levels of support and guidance.

When students see the value of assignments, especially how the content will be helpful to them now and in the future, they are more likely to be motivated to complete the tasks and put forth high levels of effort when doing so. Authentic assignments that have real-world significance can be quite motivating and engaging because students can easily see the value of the learning tasks. Faculty can share the why behind assignments, emphasizing the value of the skills and knowledge being developed to help students see the importance and relevance of learning tasks. In addition, faculty can develop assignments that mirror tasks required in various careers or even have students complete tasks needed by community partners.

Building Foundational Knowledge

Faculty use a variety of different assignments to help students achieve the course learning outcomes. Some assignments are designed to help students acquire the foundational knowledge related to the course. Foundational knowledge is needed for students to engage in more cognitively complex tasks or assignments. Formative assessments are often used for this purpose. For example, to help students learn the key concepts of the course, many faculty will require students to complete quizzes and reading assignments.

Although some may fear that quizzes are perceived negatively by students, 89% of students in Tropman's (2014) study responded that they had a very positive or somewhat positive experience with the quizzes. Students reported that quizzes encouraged them to read, and as a result they were more likely to be engaged in class discussions. Cook and Babon (2017) also found that students responded favorably to online quizzes. More specifically, students reported that weekly quizzes motivated them to engage in the readings. In addition, students indicated that knowing their classmates also did the reading increased their motivation to participate in the subsequent discussions.

In the following student story, Vidish shares how weekly quizzes prior to a lecture engaged him and helped him learn the course content.

Prelecture Quizzes
Vidish Parikh
Senior | Economics | Wilfrid Laurier University
Course: Applied Econometrics (midsized, in-person class)

My professor, Professor McCaig, designed weekly prelecture quizzes to help me track my understanding of concepts. The quizzes, which were graded, were completed online after reading a textbook chapter or engaging with an empirical paper but prior to any class discussions on the week's subject matter.

After completing the online quizzes over the weekend, the professor gave us class time to work in small groups. Our task was to complete another quiz, but this time we were permitted to pool our resources and discuss the questions with our classmates. The style and spirit of the in-class questions closely resembled the online prelecture quiz. However, the in-class quizzes were taken on scratch cards. These cards were each preloaded with the correct answers, and we had to scratch the box with the corresponding letter; if upon scratching the box a star was revealed, our selected answer was correct. This allowed me to immediately validate my learning. It also gave me multiple attempts to think critically about the correct answer, had I failed to do so on the first attempt.

After completing the scratch card quiz, the lecture became a focused class discussion. The professor nominated a member of each team to flag the most challenging questions, and these questions were discussed in depth. Quizzes motivated me to learn. Because the quizzes primarily pulled from empirical findings of research studies, I was able to directly engage with data and validate my understanding of theoretical concepts. The questions were inherently challenging, but the multiple scratch attempts prompted collaboration and reduced anxiety. These quizzes also reinforced important concepts such as how control variables work, which is important knowledge for future statisticians. I especially liked the scratch card format because of the immediate feedback. I became a better multiple-choice test taker because I was encouraged to consider why the wrong answers were wrong.

For those looking to replicate this strategy, communicate the rationale of assignments such as quizzes to students. Students will like knowing you are using a strategy that will validate their learning in an interactive format. Because there is not enough time in class to cover all topics in an in-depth manner, this approach can help you determine where to focus your energy during class so that students can develop an understanding of the important concepts in your field. You can then lecture on these issues.

❧

Online testing options such as those created by publishers make it easy for faculty to use quizzes to help students engage with content and increase learning. In addition, there are often other types of online assignments that can be used to help students develop a strong working knowledge of major concepts, theories, or research in the field. Jozwiak (2015) was found that students reported that online assignments were helpful and increased their engagement in the course. Student completion of the online assignments was also related to exam performance, with lower-achieving students benefitting the most. The benefits of online homework were also illustrated in a study by Parker and Loudon (2013). Students enrolled in an introductory-level organic chemistry class reported positive experiences with the online homework system. There was a positive correlation between engagement with online homework and course grades.

Research also supports the use of reading assignments to increase engagement and learning for students. For example, Bartolomeo-Maida (2016) evaluated the effectiveness of a journal assignment that required students to write about what they found interesting in the chapter and how the content related to their life. In addition, students had to identify questions and potential research issues related to the content of the reading. Students who completed this assignment reported high levels of engagement with the course content.

In the following student story, Elena shares how writing to learn assignments that primarily focused on the assigned readings helped her as a student.

Writing to Learn
Elena St. Amour
Sophomore | Psychology and Chemistry | Drew University
Course: Hogwarts, Houses, and Horcruxes: The Psychology of Harry Potter
(small, in-person class)

A strategy that I found engaging was the writing to learn assignment that was completed each week and was submitted online to the professor. Sometimes, the writing to learn assignment would be submitted at the end of class to summarize what had been done and discussed in class that day, but most of the time, the assignment would be a response to questions about the weekly readings. Typically, this assignment didn't take much longer than an hour to complete, as it was meant to be a brief homework assignment that would serve as a preview of what we would be covering in class. It was graded primarily based on completion.

Although the weekly writing to learn assignments were tedious at times and weren't always enjoyable to complete, they were useful because they helped me learn the material and introduced me to the concepts we would be discussing in class. Throughout the semester, these weekly assignments made it easier to participate in class and understand the progression of the course as the material we learned and discussed was integrated into each new writing to learn assignment. As a first-year student, these assignments really helped me get used to the workload of college as well as keep up in the course in which they were required.

Writing to learn assignments can easily be integrated into any type of course. Professors who want to try these assignments can consider what question prompts would work best with their assigned readings. The questions asked shouldn't be questions that take hours to respond to, as the assignment is meant to be brief and keep students centered on the key concepts from the readings so that we are ready to fully participate in class. Overall, these assignments are not difficult to grade and give students a way to stay on track in class throughout the semester.

꩜

Using Authentic Assignments to Promote Learning

Students are more likely to be engaged in the learning process when they can easily see the value of learning tasks. One of the best ways to assist students with seeing the purpose and value of tasks is through authentic assignments. Authentic assignments contextualize learning in real-world applications and can include simulated activities or tasks for community partners that are immediately used. Authentic assignments increase student engagement and learning (Brown, 2015). In an experimental study by Ozan (2019), students preparing to be teachers who completed authentic assignments, such as developing exams for use in the secondary school setting, had more positive attitudes about their learning experience and higher levels of academic performance compared to students who did not complete authentic assessments. Students in this study expressed many positive emotions including excitement because the learning experiences exposed them to their chosen profession and had real-world value.

Many faculty assign projects that represent the kinds of tasks that need to be done by employees in various careers. Examples include students majoring in education developing lesson plans, students majoring in advertising developing commercials or print advertisements, and students majoring in health sciences writing treatment plans. Assignments that require students to work in virtual teams can also mirror work-related activities. Karpova et al. (2011) found that students responded positively to a virtual collaborative project where they worked with students from three different countries to help students develop skills needed in the global apparel industry. Specifically, students found this to be a fun and enjoyable way to learn essential skills such as how to function in a virtual team with teammates from other cultures and countries and how to problem-solve and negotiate.

Social media assignments can be used in authentic ways to engage students. When students were required to use Pinterest, a social media platform, for an academic assignment they reported high levels of engagement because they saw real-world connections (Baker & Hitchcock, 2017). Research has also shown that students respond favorably to blog assignments (Cameron, 2012). Being able to write succinctly for public audiences is a skill needed in many careers.

Simulations give students the opportunity to see the impact of their actions in a real-world context. In simulated learning opportunities, students can see the positive and negative consequences of their choices and actions. This can help them learn the skills needed in a safe environment. Research shows that this type of learning can increase student engagement (Ismail & Sabapathy, 2016; Marriott et al., 2015).

In the following student story, Joseph describes a marketing simulation activity that he found to be very engaging.

Marketing Simulation
Joseph Bonacorda
Junior / Finance and Operations Management / University of Delaware
Course: Introduction to Marketing (small, in-person class)

Professor Herzenstein provided our class with access to a simulation activity where we were assigned the role of CEO of a company. We were placed into teams of four or five and assigned the goal of achieving a score of at least 75 in the simulation. The company we were assigned sold directly to other businesses and through distributors to individual customers but had been in a tailspin as of late. It was our job to readjust the marketing strategy in order to bring the company back to prosperity.

We started by watching videos to learn about the company. Information such as requirements for the products, price sensitivities, attention desired by representatives, and sales from each of the four segments of the business were provided. In addition to being provided with information on the company, we were also given valuable information on the competition. For example, we were provided with the percentage of the market held by competitors, details about their products, and pricing information.

After taking all the information provided into account, it was our responsibility to set a variety of metrics over the next 12 quarters with the goal of gaining market share and increasing revenue. We were provided with a budget that started at $800,000 per quarter and increased or decreased depending on our success. After setting each metric for the quarter, we ran the simulation and viewed the results of our decisions. We were able to see if the company earned revenue and gained market share. We were also able to see satisfaction rates and how our product compared to the competition. After reviewing and evaluating our outcomes, we adjusted the metrics before running the simulation through the next quarter. We repeated this process for all 12 quarters and then viewed our overall success.

I found this simulation to be extremely engaging and much more effective than other lessons. It was intriguing to be able to play around with the different measures and see how they impacted the company's overall standing in real time. I was also impressed with the depth and complexity of the simulation.

Most importantly, the simulation enabled us to apply concepts we had learned in class and gain insight into their true impact and function. For example, we learned in class that pricing high and offering discounts can be more effective than simply listing the price at the desired selling point. We had success using this theory in the simulation, pricing our product around $175 and offering discounts as large as 33%.

Assignments such as this one are great for helping students see the purpose of what they are learning. Practicing and understanding how to execute what we have learned effectively in a real-world context really helps us understand the material. Additionally, having an assignment that can be approached in many ways is very useful. Being able to apply your knowledge as you see fit is more effective than being guided to a predetermined solution. Students were able to apply different schools of thought, learn from mistakes, and implement various strategies until they found success. It was very difficult to achieve a score above 75, so students were really forced to refine their knowledge and develop a truly effective marketing strategy before experiencing success. These factors combined led this assignment to be one of the more impactful and effective assignments I have completed as a student. I would recommend faculty look for similar, challenging assignments that enable students to apply their knowledge in creative ways in a real-world context.

❧

Although activities such as simulations can motivate some students, it may not motivate others. Rogmans and Abaza (2019) found that although highly motivated students became even more engaged after participating in simulations, this was not the case for students who had lower levels of motivation. Students who entered the course with lower levels of motivation became less engaged, noting that the simulation exercise was complex. Peng and Abdullah (2018) found that simulations worked better in online versus face-to-face classes and discovered a gender gap, with males performing better than females.

The findings from these studies remind us that different types of assignments can affect students in different ways. Ensuring that students have strong foundational knowledge before engaging in simulations is important. In addition, providing students with detailed instructions is also helpful. Perhaps most importantly, faculty can provide high levels of support and guidance to ensure that students will believe in their ability to complete the complicated task and will be successful at the task. This can increase the likelihood that all students will benefit from the simulated learning experience.

Another type of authentic assignment is one that serves the needs of a community partner. Students exhibit high levels of engagement when they are working on an assignment that serves the community. This was demonstrated in a study by Wollschleger (2019). In this study, student engagement and learning increased for students in an undergraduate applied research class who were required to conduct research projects for community partners as compared to students who developed skills through simulated activities. Students found it very rewarding that community partner organizations were benefitting from their work. This was also illustrated in a study by Croes and Visser (2015) where students competed in a Google marketing campaign. The results of this study indicated that students appreciated the opportunity to work directly with a company and liked that the task was different from many of their other assignments. In addition to engaging students, results also demonstrated that this activity helped students develop interpersonal and intrapersonal skills, digital technical skills, and flexibility and adaptability. These are all essential skills that employers value.

In the following student story, Kaitlynn talks about how developing a sexual education curriculum was engaging, because she was creating something that community members could benefit from.

Creating Sexual Education Curricula
Kaitlynn Ely
Graduate student | International Studies | Muhlenberg College
Course: Psychology of Women (small, in-person class)

In my Psychology of Women course, the class was split into four groups for our final project. Our task was to create new, engaging sexual education curricula for an assigned age group (children, adolescents, young adults, and aging). Each group had to investigate the biological, social, psychological, spiritual, cognitive, developmental, behavioral, identity, and power influences on sexuality for their age group. To begin brainstorming, our professor wrote each of the nine topic areas on a large piece of paper and taped them around the room. The class broke into groups of three or four and performed a round-robin, writing down everything that came to mind when we read the listed topic area. For example, under "biological," we wrote terms such as *reproductive system*, *hormones*, and *puberty*, and under the "power" category, we wrote words such as *rape, straight,* and *White.* After 5 minutes, we rotated around the room to read ideas already written and added to the list.

After collecting peer-reviewed sources and researching sexual education lessons, we developed and presented our new curricula to the psychology department. As you would expect, our group that focused on aging developed a curriculum that addressed menopause, femininity, motherhood, divorce, and sexual intercourse among older adults. The curriculum for the children cohort looked quite different and focused on reproductive system terminology and puberty.

My professor allowed us to explore sexual education in a new way, thinking about what different populations need. Most women are not told about menopause and the changes their bodies will encounter until it's happening. And many women lose their sense of sexuality and femininity postmenopause, making it difficult for this community to have a healthy sex life with their partners.

The most engaging part of this project was knowing that this curriculum can not only be taught but also help a lot of people understand their bodies, emotions, and feelings more clearly. The aging community, specifically, is often a group left out of the sexuality conversation. It was a good feeling to know that while this project was a part of the class, I was creating something that could be used to educate this community.

ॐ

Another way to bring real-world value front and center is by creating assignments that directly relate to the students' place of employment. This makes the connection between academia and career much more visible and transparent. For example, faculty might ask students to evaluate current processes and determine strategies for improvements or encourage students to draft documents and resources or even develop programs that relate to their current place of employment. Students place a high value on learning tasks that can easily apply to careers (Rodriguez & Koubek, 2019).

In the example that follows, Carrie, a graduate student who is working full time and is also a mother of two, describes how an assignment that required her to develop a proposal for a new program at her place of employment increased her engagement. The fact that this proposal was well received and implemented by upper-level administration was particularly rewarding to her.

Developing a Proposal
Carrie Hachadurian
Graduate student, mother of two who is employed full time /
Higher Education Student Affairs / Western Carolina University
Course: Organization, Administration, and Finance in Higher Education
(small, in-person class)

In the Organization, Administration, and Finance in Higher Education class, Professor Yancey Gulley challenged us to create a mock proposal to either change an existing program or process or create an entirely new program or process in our respective departments. I work full time in a career development office that currently oversees the student employment hiring and onboarding processes (tax and confidentiality forms, federal form I-9 creation and updates, direct deposit, and time sheet creation). I developed a proposal to move this function from the Career Development Office to the Office of Human Resources, where it better aligns with their mission and existing resources. This is something our office has tried to do in the past, but these efforts were not previously successful.

Even though this was an assignment I needed to complete, I used the opportunity to tangibly and strategically propose this institutional change. I used classroom discussions and readings to analyze the departmental mission and vision statements and articulate current issues related to the institutional liability of housing student hiring and onboarding practices in the Career Development office. I also analyzed current employee flow charts of both the Career Development office and the Human Resources Department and researched where student employment hiring is housed at other institutions. After thoroughly exploring the issues and practices at other institutions, I proposed changes to work responsibilities in the Human Resources Department. The proposal included anticipated costs associated with making the change as well as anticipated results or implications from implementing the change. I am ecstatic to report that my proposal was received well by upper administration and that the university approved and implemented this change.

This assignment was engaging for me because it was practical rather than hypothetical. It empowered and motivated me to create a proposal that had the chance of making an actual change at the university. My full-time position at the university is entry level, and if I did not have this assignment, I would not have felt qualified to create the proposal. As a student, I am much more engaged in assignments that are tangible and practical in nature rather than hypothetical or what I would call "busy work." I especially liked this assignment because we were forced to look at our own departments and develop something new. As we went through the process, we were making connections among class discussions, readings, and our actual work environments.

My advice to faculty wishing to create meaningful class assignments is to make assignments practical, tangible, and challenging. Students enjoy creating a product, especially if that product could be pitched to become a reality. I firmly believe students can do much more than they think they can; sometimes they just need the push and encouragement to make it happen.

❧

Getting students involved in on-campus projects and experiences is another way to engage students through authentic assignments. When students get to plan and implement programs or events on campus, they are learning essential skills while benefitting their own institution. This approach also enables students to see the fruits of their labor. Students will undoubtedly enjoy seeing the success of an event or program that they helped plan and implement.

In the following student story, Jaclyn describes the benefit of being part of a team that planned the career fair on campus.

Planning a Career Fair
Jaclyn Bonacorda
Senior / Event Management and Hospitality Management / University of Central Florida
Course: Event Operations (small, in-person class)

One of the electives available for event management majors at Rosen College is Event Operations. This class provides students with the opportunity to get hands-on experience in event planning and operations by being involved with the Rosen College Career Fair. The Rosen College Career Fair is held each fall and spring semester and gives all Rosen students the opportunity to connect with over 100 hospitality companies looking to hire students for various types of positions. Our class was divided into four departments: décor/food and beverage, marketing, exhibition services, and procurement, all led by a student leader and coleader and supervised by Professor Brinkman.

We worked from the beginning of the fall semester (late August) to the event date (November 8) to create a theme, menu, marketing materials, floor plan, and more for the Career Fair. We worked with multiple Rosen staff members such as the controller, head chef, and event manager to make sure everything was done correctly and to standard. We also had to work with outside vendors such as a general contractor, who provided the booths for vendors, and printing companies for our marketing materials. On the day of the Career Fair, we were all on campus from 5:00 a.m. until 4:00 p.m. We also hosted pre- and postevent meetings with all the Rosen staff involved in the event.

This semester-long assignment was extremely meaningful because it provided us with experience in planning an event from start to finish, something a lot of us don't always have the chance to do while in school. It's one thing to sit in a classroom and learn about event management and what we should do once we're in the "real world," but it is another to actually be a part of that process and learn from the experience of doing it. The fact that this was a real event helped me and my classmates stay motivated because we knew there was no room for error. While doing a project about a hypothetical event, or any other situation, it can be easy to gloss over something that may seem insignificant. However, when it comes to planning a real event, everything must be considered and cannot simply be skipped over. This reality gave us a reason to work hard to ensure our Career Fair was the best yet.

I would encourage colleges and faculty to try and implement classes that give students a chance to gain real-world experience in their field, as this class did. These experiences are engaging and excellent ways for us to develop our skills. If this is not possible, professors can also create projects in their classes to try and mimic real-world experiences to help students get a feel for what the "real world" in their field is like.

∽⚬∾

Pushing Students Outside Their Comfort Zone

Learning often requires challenging students to move outside their comfort zone. Research has consistently shown that challenging tasks and goals result in higher levels of effort and achievement (Locke & Latham, 2002) and that the brain responds in an engaging way to new or novel tasks or situations (Cell Press, 2006). Patel (2016) discusses how being uncomfortable and trying out new tasks or being in different situations can result in increased learning and growth.

Faculty can use a variety of assignments to stretch students to engage in behaviors or activities that they wouldn't typically do. Providing students with a clear rationale for the task, including the goals and objectives, and supporting them can increase the likelihood that students will find value in activities that push them beyond their comfort zone.

In the student example that follows, Kayla describes how her professor pushed her beyond her comfort zone. Specifically, she shares how her professor helped her become more comfortable speaking up in class and how this was beneficial to her.

Speaking Up in Class
Kayla Wathen
Sophomore | Biology | Middlesex County College
Course: General Biology I (small, in-person class)

As a Middlesex County College student, I have had positive interactions with many different professors. However, with Professor Gardner, I feel that I have achieved goals that I never even thought possible. In my very first semester here, I had the privilege of being enrolled in her General Biology I lecture and lab course. I had an idea that I wanted to do something with science, but coming out of high school I wasn't so sure of my capabilities to flourish in this area of study.

As a first-year student, I was unaware of the amount of work that would be required of me in college and what I would be expected to do. I wasn't always comfortable exploring new things such as developing new study habits, forming study groups, and making connections with fellow classmates and professors. I had not previously had classroom experiences that required so much active participation. I tend to be more on the shy side, especially when it comes to pursuing something new and different.

Professor Gardner pushed me outside of my comfort zone by expecting me and the other students to be vocal and involved during the lecture. Part of our final grade was participation. She taught us how to be good students. She often brought in her own notes and study guides that she created when she was a college student. She made sure we all felt comfortable enough to stop her during the lecture if we had any questions or needed clarification on a specific subject. Professor Gardner also encouraged students to have educated discussions with her outside of class. These conversations encouraged me to become educated on real-world topics that coincided with what we were learning and be able to apply that to a real conversation. As a result, I became very comfortable asking questions in front of her and the class. This was vital for my success in the course. To this day, I still use a lot of these skills that she showed me when I first started college.

Professor Gardner made it very clear that she wants us all to reach our highest potential, and for us to do so we have to be confident students willing to be pushed outside of our comfort zone. I honestly did not see myself being the student who was outspoken and vocal in class, but now I am. I never realized how much that would help me be successful. Professor Gardner helped me see how beneficial skills like these are in not only my classes but also the real world and future jobs.

For faculty who want to push students to find their voice and participate in discussions, help students feel comfortable. It's important for everyone to feel safe and confident enough to have a conversation with each other and the professor. Making participation an important part of the grade can provide students with an incentive. I wanted to do well and found myself getting more involved with my fellow classmates as well as with the professor and the lesson. It kept me engaged the whole time and kept me focused on what we were learning.

❧

In Kayla's example, the professor provided encouragement and support that helped her become more comfortable getting uncomfortable. This is important as students will need support as they step outside their comfort zone.

In the next student example, Brett also shares how his professor supported and challenged him to stretch himself. Brett's professor pushed him to write in a different genre, and he appreciated being challenged to do so. As a result, he gained confidence in his ability. This example reminds us that even students who are generally confident can become uncomfortable when confronted with a new task.

New Forms of Writing
Brett Hurst
Graduate student / English / The University of Alabama at Birmingham
Course: Creative Nonfiction Workshop (small, in-person class)

My writing life before the creative nonfiction writing class was filled with stories that stemmed from my imagination. Little did I know that this immersive journalism assignment from a creative nonfiction class would become one of the most rewarding assignments I had ever done in my academic career. It allowed me to express myself through a different genre as well as widen the scope of my writing abilities. Professor Kerry Madden-Lunsford used many tools to engage me in having full confidence with this assignment. First, she gave me the freedom to write about what I wanted. Sure, there were guidelines to follow, but it was all in my hands as far as picking my "subject." To me, this assignment was about removing the idea of writing strictly about myself and getting used to delving into another person's life.

It was a tradition in the nonfiction workshop for students to complete the semester by doing an immersion journalism piece. As a prominent writer of fiction, the beginning stages of this assignment left me clueless. I understood that I had to seek out someone to interview and then write about their profession and overall experience. This was a perfect opportunity to go back and visit my science teacher. The interview was natural to me, and I asked questions that I came up with on the spot. I felt like I had a talk show for a minute, and that was enough to boost my confidence.

I chose to do something more interesting than interviewing someone with a cool job for the second time around. At the time, my close friend was in a relationship, and I wanted to ask them one simple question: Why? Why were they in a long-term relationship, and could they convince me to be in one? This immersion journalism piece felt more comedic because I would tell jokes to try to make them share their story. Writing the outcome and the experience was fun for me, and it felt more like a hobby, like a piece of writing for myself rather than for a grade.

The last experience was when I interviewed the medical examiner of my hometown. We arranged a meeting in his office, where he explained to me his profession and duties. This interview impacted me the most because it made me want to write about not only my experience interviewing him but also a piece on the life of a medical examiner. This content was excellent starting material for a fiction short story, and it helped me complete my third assignment.

After I earned my undergraduate degree, I began wondering why this one assignment had such an impact on me. Writing, no matter what genre, is a universal tool in a writer's tool kit. The common thread between nonfiction and fiction, for me at least, was that a lot of my fiction was based on nonfictional situations. Without doing this assignment and talking to authentic people, I would not have the foundational means to start and complete future short stories.

If my workshop community in this class was negative and hostile, I probably would have been nervous about sharing my work with them. Luckily, my professor established a positive and charming environment to ensure all her students felt safe. If I had to give one piece of advice to anyone wanting to endorse this assignment, it would be to allow students to have as much creative freedom as possible.

৵৵

Faculty can also help students move beyond their comfort zone with assignments that require students to interact with others through on- and off-campus events and activities that they probably would not have participated in if not required to do so. Participating in events and activities can help students develop essential interpersonal and communication skills while also learning course content. Although students may find many of these tasks uncomfortable at first, at the end of the semester students will often report that the task was not only engaging but also very helpful to them in their learning journey.

For many students, interacting and working with others from different racial and cultural backgrounds may be a new experience, especially if they grew up in a homogeneous neighborhood. Shin (2011) found that an assignment requiring students taking an art class to informally interact with diverse members of the community gave students an opportunity to learn about race, ethnicity, and culture and dispelled inaccurate perceptions and biases. Kurpis and Hunter (2017) also found that an assignment that required students to interview someone from a different culture about consumer behaviors increased student motivation, confidence in their ability to communicate effectively with individuals from different cultural backgrounds, and cultural knowledge.

In the following example, Cayleigh shares how much she enjoyed and valued an assignment that required her to learn about different cultures through an interview and related research project.

Cultural Interview and Research Project
Cayleigh Keenan
Senior | Elementary Education | William Paterson University
Course: Diversity and Equity in Schools (small, in-person class)

In my Diversity and Equity in Schools course, we had to identify someone who attended school in an environment that was very different from the one we experienced. In addition to focusing on the sociocultural conditions related to the school and community setting, we were also encouraged to identify a person who had different family and cultural experiences. We were expected to consider the differences in our family and community life and how these experiences may have impacted our educational experiences. In addition to the personal information we learned from the interviewee, we also conducted research to learn more about the school, school district, and town itself. The final project consisted of a research paper and a presentation that we shared with our class.

Learning about someone else's cultural and educational upbringing is engaging because it gives you an opportunity to step outside of the bubble you grew up in and see the social and educational experiences of others. This assignment gave us an opportunity to see real-life examples of what we had learned, opening our eyes to various perspectives and experiences. This project really helped me stay motivated toward my goal of becoming an educator because I was able to clearly see the educational gaps in our country through personal stories. It left me motivated to work at reducing these educational gaps.

Implementing this type of project is extremely beneficial for the students in the class. It helped me better understand how significantly different the educational experience can be for students living in the same area or state. When attempting to use a project like this, I would recommend having connections to people who would be willing to be interviewed by your students. Being a resource for your students for this project is critical. Direction and guidance can help students figure out what to focus on when gathering information.

⌘

Although much can be learned from conversations with others from different cultural backgrounds, faculty can stretch students even further by requiring them to attend a religious or cultural event or activity. Experiencing the culture is very different from just hearing about it. Alexandrin et al. (2008) report that students who were required to attend cultural events outside of their comfort zone found this experience to be very valuable. For example, a student who grew up in a family that did not support gay marriage attended a pro same-sex marriage rally at the capitol building and reported that participating in this event helped her see the similarities between homosexual and heterosexual couples.

In the following student story, Benjamin shares how powerful it was for him to attend an unfamiliar religious service.

Experiencing a Different Religion
Benjamin Sackler
Senior | Political Science | College of Charleston
Course: Religion in American Politics (small, in-person class)

We live in a time of intolerance and stigmatization against those who fall in the category of "other." Historically, the United States has prided itself on acceptance; supposedly, anyone, regardless of circumstances and social identity or background, can become something in this country. However, this sentiment hides the misfortunes of marginalized groups who have struggled for equality since America's creation. Encouraged by even the top political leaders of America, some are still targeted today, subjected to hate and disgust from their fellow Americans. This narrative of prejudice expressed by the top spreads to the masses, causing Americans to internalize a level of fear and dislike that they believe they are supposed to have against certain groups.

Religious discrimination has been especially widespread in the United States in the past several years. Islamophobia, anti-Semitism, and other forms of discrimination have dominated news headlines, polarizing our nation and barring forward progress toward social harmony. Professor Shyam Sriram, who taught my Religion in American Politics class at the College of Charleston (and who has since moved to Butler University), identified this as a learning opportunity for students. By assigning students to attend a religious service of a religion the student did not grow up in, Professor Sriram was giving us the opportunity to experience something that we had never before experienced as well as showing that our prejudices are extremely irrational.

Professor Sriram provided the class with an extensive list of places of worship organized by religion in Charleston or nearby. However, students could complete this assignment anywhere. During the service, we were instructed to engage with leaders of the place of worship we chose, as well as others in the congregation. Additionally, we were to actively engage with the service itself, using active listening skills as well as respect. Following the service, we had to write a reflection paper. The reflection consisted of an account of our interactions with the leaders of the place of worship and the congregation members, as well as an objective and emotional account of the service. Students visited all types of places of worship, from mosques to synagogues to Unitarian Universalist churches.

This assignment was so effective and engaging because it forced us out of our comfort zone. In these troubling times of intolerance, there are many, of course, who desire to be on the right side of history. However, it is sometimes difficult for people to take the extra step of learning about other cultures, belief systems, and ways of life. This step is extremely important for furthering progressivism in the category of religious acceptance. Professor Sriram's assignment allowed us to understand that we are all more similar than we perceive ourselves to be.

I encourage all professors to push their students out of their comfort zones if they want students to have a truly impactful experience. Whether it's through class discussion or assignments such as this one, students must be encouraged to interact with material that makes them uncomfortable in order to be active citizens. Through this activity, I was exposed to a facet of life I would not have been otherwise exposed to, and for that I am thankful.

ॐ

Fostering Creativity

Assignments that foster creativity have numerous benefits, including increased student engagement and learning. Based on a national study of seniors at 227 different colleges, Miller (2018) found that

> even after controlling for several demographic and institutional characteristics, creative coursework is a significant positive predictor of confidence in several different skills and abilities that are important for adapting to traditional and non-traditional work settings, including creative thinking, critical thinking, entrepreneurial skills, and networking abilities. (p. 88)

Many assignments have rigid guidelines and may not offer students the chance to engage in creative thought and actions. Although students do appreciate clear explanations and guidelines about what is expected, students will also value assignments that foster creativity. Creative assignments enable students to approach tasks in different ways. As a result, students can build on their strengths. In the student story that follows, Julie shares how having creative freedom with an assignment was engaging and empowering.

Creative Essay Portfolio
Julie Bechtel Patino
Senior / Secondary English Education / New Jersey City University
Course: Children's and Young Adult Literature (small, in-person class)

It's crazy how fast learning can leak out of the brain. The more that is crammed into memory, the faster the information seems to gush out—unless the teacher makes the material meaningful and the assessments authentic. I believe this process of weaving content together and keeping students engaged is the greatest challenge professors face. Here's how one of my professors met this challenge head-on.

As is customary, on the very first day of Children's and Young Adult Literature, Professor Giunta went through the class syllabus: weekly process journal, four mini essays, three presentations, a larger reflective essay, and a revised final project. Immediately, I jumped to the conclusion that this professor wanted to stuff as much busy work as she could down our throats before we escaped her clutches. While I was making this silent judgment, she explained the nature of the final project. We would be writing a summative document drawing from all the expertise and knowledge accumulated in class, and, furthermore, we could pick what type of essay we wished to write. On paper, these two statements don't look revolutionary, but they are, because they established two important concepts in my mind: *All class material is pertinent to my final goal* and *I can guide this project in a personally relevant way.* The workload did not change, but now I believed that the assignments would be meaningful and worthwhile.

One recommended format for the final project was the creative essay of a fictional story. I chose this option. We would be reading and dissecting children's and young adult novels in class, and by creating my own story I knew I could showcase a full portfolio of my knowledge with my single creative essay. The creative aspect of plot and character would be my own ideas, but in class I would gain the necessary tools with which to evaluate my project. As we explored different works, I made note of the connections and aspects emphasized by the professor. I then examined my project against my notes.

Although this final project afforded us much freedom, it also had a definitive structure. Professor Giunta required a project proposal, updates, conferences in her office, and an abstract that explained the project's relevance to the class. She was serious about her students' progress and output, and this pushed us to emulate this commitment. At the end of the semester, I received a great grade on my final project. I was pleased. I felt that I had learned better how to evaluate and teach children's and young adult literature, and I also had tangible proof of my progress. Inevitably, I will forget a significant portion of Professor Giunta's teaching, but compared to many other college classes, I believe I have retained and used much of what I learned that semester.

〰️

As Julie shared, students often invest more when assignments foster creative thinking and processes. This will typically result in higher levels of engagement during the learning process but also in learning that lasts over time.

In the next student story, Kristina, a first-generation graduate student, shares how creativity in an assignment paved the way for her to think more deeply about her research interests.

Creativity in Assignments
Kristina M. Perrelli
First-generation graduate student, mother of three, who is employed
full time / Education / University of Rhode Island
Course: Core Seminar in Education: Thinking and Reasoning
(small, in-person class)

One of the courses that really stands out to me is one where the professor used creative teaching strategies and assignments. We had two core assignments in this course: The first was to develop a research idea and methodology, and the second was to create a conceptual model or map of our research plan. What made this project different was that we did not have to ground our work in previous scholarship. Instead, we were encouraged to imagine all the possible ways we might approach our topic and what we might learn from the topic and the process of conducting the research.

We were all studying education. In my study, I knew I would be engaging with people who would share their life experiences. Writing about a research idea without worrying about citations pushed my thinking to areas I would have never explored had I needed to provide scholarly support for each idea. I was free to imagine how participants in my study might respond to the questions I asked them and what I would learn from their responses. I was able to think about why I cared about the topic.

We were told to create a conceptual model of our study, but we were not given specific instructions on how to create the model. In our class of nine, each of us had a very different conceptual model. One student chose to play a game with the class to help us conceptualize her research idea and plan. This assignment allowed me to visualize—not just write about—my ideas. I used different shapes and colors to show the relationships among the major constructs (or key parts) of my study. I also used linear and nonlinear arrows to show the paths the study might take depending on the decisions I made as a researcher and what was shared by participants.

The teaching and learning strategies of this course were engaging and motivating because they provided me with the freedom to explore my ideas without being constrained by the rules of academia. It is important and necessary to ground ideas in scholarship, but this course provided something even more significant: space to think creatively about and imagine how I might contribute to my field. It also gave me strategies I continue to use to push along my thinking or writing when I feel stuck in the process.

I encourage faculty—of all disciplines—to think about how they might incorporate teaching and learning strategies that foster imagination and creativity in students. What would that course or assignment look like? Are there barriers that typically occur in courses or doctoral work that can be removed to help students explore their ideas more freely? What would your students gain from using their imaginations to conceptualize their research ideas? How can you provide an educational space that gives students the freedom to creatively develop a research plan?

∞

Giving students the freedom of choice opens the door for creativity to be fostered. It can also be an excellent way to increase engagement. Not surprisingly, students will be more invested in topics that they care about. An added benefit is that this creates a classroom culture where the professor gets to know students and what matters to them. Students also get to know one another.

This was particularly important to Kara. In the following student story, Kara shares how the freedom to creatively approach written and oral tasks in a speech class helped her find her voice.

Finding My Voice
Kara Infelise
Returning adult sophomore | Graphic Communications
Gateway Technical College
Course: Public Speaking (small, in-person class)

When I think of influential professors that I've been blessed to have in my life, one person in particular comes to mind. Her perseverance and dedication to inclusivity and genuine care about her students on such a deep level have had a significant impact on my life, and for that I am grateful. Professor Hankins was my speech professor, a class I was so unsure of in the beginning. But I quickly fell in love with it because of the passion that Professor Hankins brought into the classroom. What I really enjoyed was that every assignment was made so that whatever we wrote about meant something to us as the student. We had the freedom to choose topics that mattered to us. Because she designed the course in this way, each and everyone one of her students poured their hearts and soul into their assignments.

In one of the first assignments, we had to introduce ourselves through a brief speech. When I introduced myself and included that I'm also Mexican, Native American, and a lesbian, Professor Hankins didn't even blink an eye throughout the entire speech. Instead, my introductory speech was met with smiles and enthusiasm for being so open and speaking in such an eloquent way. From introductory speeches to persuasive and informative ones, we had free reign to explore topics and pick something we were passionate about. One day, Professor Hankins even had us meet at a park to take a walk around, stretch our legs, and discuss topics of our choice for an upcoming informational speech.

Throughout the semester she was there if I had any questions about anything, had my back when I was met with adversity and intolerance in another class, and instilled a deeper love of writing and even a passion for public speaking. By allowing us to choose a topic to write about and present, she allowed us to be authentically ourselves and created an environment where it wasn't just about learning how to write. We really got to know one another in this class, and we learned how to find our voice and present it in the best way possible. Being able to present yourself well matters, and these experiences helped me gain confidence and skills that will help me in the future. And for someone like me, a gay woman of color, finding that voice has been an invaluable lesson.

ॐ

Service-Learning

"Service-learning incorporates community work into the curriculum, giving students real-world learning experiences that enhance their academic learning while providing a tangible benefit for the community" (Campus Compact, n.d., para. 1). The value of service-learning has consistently been demonstrated. Students report many benefits of participating in service-learning, such as enhanced leadership skills, the learning of practical skills needed in the workplace, increased self-confidence, and a greater understanding of cultural and racial differences (Caspersz & Olaru, 2017). Service-learning has also been connected to academic learning, personal growth, and higher levels of civic responsibility (Wang & Calvano, 2018). Students have higher levels of enjoyment in classes with service-learning as compared to classes without service-learning (Fleck et al., 2017).

Service-learning is an excellent way to engage students with not only course content but also the community. However, it is important to note that service-learning requires careful and intentional course design and planning. Collaboration with the service-learning office on campus is critical as it can help faculty develop a deep understanding of service-learning models and processes, as well as assist faculty with developing strong partnerships with community organizations. While most of the strategies described throughout this book are relatively easy to implement, the suggestions provided in this section on service-learning are much grander in scale and thus will require significant collaboration and planning prior to being implemented.

In a fascinating study, Chan et al. (2019) investigated whether mandatory service-learning had positive outcomes. Despite controversial opinions about this issue in the field, the results of this study suggest that mandatory service-learning can be valuable, as indicated by students' perceived value and academic performance. What mattered more than whether the experience was mandatory or voluntary though was the quality of the learning experience.

There are many ways that faculty can incorporate service-learning into courses. Faculty may choose to have a required service-learning project or may include an option of service-learning among a menu of other assignment options. The key is that the tasks need to align with the course learning outcomes while also serving a need in the community.

Faculty who wish to use a service-learning approach should reach out to the experts on their campus for assistance. In most cases, faculty will need to spend a significant amount of time, usually at least one semester, learning and planning in order to effectively implement a service-learning component into a course. Although implementing service-learning is a huge investment of time on the part of the faculty member, there is typically a high return on investment as student engagement and learning will undoubtedly increase.

In the following example, Davis highlights the value of participating in a service-learning project.

Service-Learning at an Assisted Living Facility
Davis Wilson
Graduate student / Higher Education and Student Affairs
Western Carolina University
Course: Recreational Therapy for Older Adults (small, in-person class)

During this class, we focused on using assessments and interventions to help the geriatric population in recreation therapy. To achieve this, our professor reached out and partnered with one of the local assisted living facilities in the community. The class went to the assisted living facility each week to conduct group interventions and work on a one-to-one basis with our assigned resident. For the case study project, our task was to get to know the resident by using recreational therapy assessments. This allowed us to get to know our residents better while applying knowledge that we were learning in the classroom.

Being able to go to the assisted living facility once a week was one of the best experiences I have ever had for a class. It brought me just as much joy as it did my assigned resident. It was great to bring smiles to the faces of residents while learning at the same time. The assignments we had throughout the semester, such as progress notes and the case summary, helped me see the connection between the service and learning in the class.

Service-learning is a great way for students to make a difference in the community. For faculty wanting to use service-learning as part of their course, I would recommend that they find a way to make the experience enjoyable for students but at the same time challenging. It is also important that students see the value and meaning of the tasks.

☙❧

As Davis described, there are many benefits to service-learning projects. It was one of the most memorable learning experiences for him, and he reported that it really helped him learn the content. Both he and his assigned resident also enjoyed spending time together.

Service-learning opportunities provide deep learning experiences that help students learn essential skills and knowledge. In the next student example, Rosemary shares how memorable and engaging her service-learning experience was for her.

Designing a Sustainable Pub
Rosemary Brockett
Junior / Environmental Studies / Wilfrid Laurier University
Course: Introduction to Sustainability (midsized, in-person class)

When I registered for a course called Introduction to Sustainability, I thought the coursework would be quite boring and theoretical, likely approaching the problems from an intellectual standpoint and from a distance—as learning often is at a university. However, I was wonderfully surprised to discover that Professor McLeman went to great lengths and gave considerable thought to develop assignments that would engage us in a meaningful, interactive, and challenging way. By the end, this course was one of the best ones I had taken.

As a class, Professor McLeman had us partner with the local township of Ayr, Ontario. We were tasked to develop proposed solutions to the various sustainability challenges facing the town. We had to address issues related to economic prosperity, suburb development, road traffic, social integration, and poorly utilized environmental features. It began by busing our class out to the town, in mid-Canadian winter, to walk around in −20°C weather, seeing the place we were trying to help. We met the local administrator and heard from community members and stakeholders. This helped us understand the community and the struggles they were facing and allowed us to begin developing assignment proposals to revive aspects of the community.

In my group, we chose to tackle aspects of social, economic, and environmental sustainability by designing a proposal for a new beer pub. The town had recently lost its social hub with the closing of an old inn, and we wanted to revive this with a trendy new family-friendly pub. The pub would capitalize on the local millpond and the newest sustainable methods of brewing and cooking to grow the heart of the town around sustainable values and community. We researched real estate options, priced out brewing equipment, planned a closed-loop system for brewing waste, and looked for investors. We ensured the pub's unique location and focus would encapsulate sustainable ideals and appeal to the community and the broader region.

At the end of the course, we presented our proposal, along with many others from the rest of our class, to the administrator, stakeholders, and community members. We hoped that some form of our projects might be implemented by the community in the coming years. Being able to work with a tangible community, one we walked around and one in which we talked to the residents, made the assignments of this course worthwhile and meaningful. I really got to see how the principles and ideals of sustainability I was studying played out in real life and in the context of many other often competing factors. Having a personal perspective on the nuances and challenges of applying concepts made them memorable and more useful.

For professors wanting to engage students through assignments, I recommend giving your students something meaningful and impactful to do. Activities such as this make us feel like we have something of value to offer with the hours we put into our coursework. Take us to visit and see what we are researching and writing about. Then it becomes real, interesting, and meaningful. As a result, we will participate, do high-quality work, and be engaged.

☙❧

Service-learning projects are most likely to engage students when they are designed well. This is why it's so critical to partner with professionals in the service-learning office. Ngai et al. (2018) conducted a study with over 2,000 students to determine what factors related to the service-learning project most influenced successful outcomes. Results revealed that service-learning projects that involved challenging and meaningful tasks and were perceived to be beneficial to the community were most effective. Students also discussed the importance of being prepared for the service activity. In other words, students need to know about the community they will be serving and have the necessary background knowledge and skills for the task at hand.

It is important to recognize that participating in service-learning may benefit some students more than others. In a research study conducted by Seider et al. (2013), it was found that White students benefitted more than students of color. Although students of color did acknowledge positive experiences with service-learning, their descriptions were more moderate in nature compared to White students' descriptions. Interview responses revealed that some students of color were hesitant to contribute to conversations because they didn't want to represent their race and were uncomfortable doing so in an environment where there was an obvious racial divide, with people they were serving being mostly people of color while the students were predominantly White.

As much of the learning that stems from service-learning comes from reflection and discussion, it is critical for faculty to develop safe spaces for students to have open dialogues about their learning experiences. Seider et al. (2013) suggest having conversations about race, culture, and class early in the semester, encouraging students to recognize the position they each bring to the service-learning placement. It is also important to help students develop respectful vocabulary and to consider how their messages may be perceived by others. Based on a literature review, Cate and Russ-Eft (2018) reported that the key elements of service-learning programs that worked well for Latinx students include "(a) integration of social support networks; (b) social consciousness-raising, identity exploration; and (c) peer-to-peer mentoring situations" (p. 224). Thus, in addition to building in safe spaces for conversations, faculty who want to ensure that all students benefit will also want to incorporate support structures. Faculty development related to service-learning also needs to focus on fostering an inclusive learning environment and how to have courageous conversations about race, ethnicity, and equity.

Faculty Reflection Questions

1. What assignments can I use to build foundational knowledge so that students build self-efficacy?

2. How can I clearly communicate the rationale and expectations of my assignments?

3. How authentic are the assignments in my course? What opportunities are there for more authentic assignments?

4. What simulations are available? How can assignments benefit community partners?

5. How do I challenge students with my assignments? What assignments can I develop to push students outside of their comfort zone?

6. What supports will I need to provide to help students take on these challenges and be successful?

7. How can I give students more opportunities to foster their creativity through my assignments?

8. What opportunities are there for service-learning in my courses? How can I support all students, especially students of color, with these learning experiences?

5

FEEDBACK

Feedback is one of the most powerful ways faculty can help students learn and develop skills. Feedback can motivate students because it validates efforts made and provides guidance on how to improve (Nicol & Macfarlane-Dick, 2006). Although students report finding praise to be emotionally pleasing, it is not always perceived as helpful. Students report that positive feedback is often generic in nature (e.g., "Good work") and that this type of feedback doesn't often lead to increased efforts (Lipnevich & Smith, 2009). Constructive feedback, in contrast, is very useful because it provides students with guidance about how to improve. Feedback that connects to a standard and is specific and constructive is especially helpful in the learning process (Wlodkowski, 2008).

Unfortunately, faculty feedback practices do not always match what is recommended. Prompt feedback was one of the seven principles for good undergraduate teaching shared in Chickering and Gamson's (1987) seminal work, and students report really appreciating frequent, genuine feedback (Mushi, 2001). Prompt feedback best enables students to learn from comments and suggestions and is highly valued by students (Rodriguez & Koubek, 2019). However, many students report not receiving feedback in a timely manner. According to a national survey, only slightly over half of the students who responded to the survey indicated that faculty provided prompt feedback on assignments (McClenney, 2007).

When feedback is provided to students, faculty are often focusing on technical issues rather than providing high-level guidance about how to improve their work product. This was illustrated in a study by Stern and Solomon (2006). After randomly selecting students, the researchers analyzed their portfolios, which contained all the papers they wrote in college along with the feedback provided on each paper. Most of the feedback addressed grammar, punctuation, paragraph and sentence structure, and word choice. Only 6% of the assignments reviewed offered scholarly advice. The sheer number of comments about technical errors can communicate to students that these skills are the most important ones. Although technical skills are important to develop, faculty will likely be most interested in students developing higher-level skills such as the ability to clearly communicate ideas, ground ideas in theory and research, and critically evaluate information. Patchan et al. (2016) found that the quality of future products is higher when students act on feedback that is focused on substance. Thus, it's important for faculty to provide feedback that helps them focus their attention on the big picture.

Faculty can draw attention to essential high-level skills by focusing their feedback on progress related to these skills. Writing comments that address the overall work and placing these comments at the top of the paper can bring attention to what matters most. Phillips and Wolcott (2014) conducted an interesting study on the placement of feedback. In this study on undergraduate accounting students, feedback shared in a summary format versus being interspersed throughout the paper benefitted the midlevel students the most, but the lowest-performing students benefitted more from feedback throughout the paper. The highest-performing students benefitted equally from both approaches. Thus, it is important to consider the audience when providing feedback.

Patchan et al. (2016) found that students are less likely to act on high-level feedback than specific, localized feedback. This research finding suggests that faculty will need to provide guidance and support on how to act on this high-level suggestion. In other words, high-level feedback may work best if it includes suggested actions. For example, if a paper lacks an effective organizational structure, it can be helpful to provide students with tools such as outline or mapping techniques to review and think through the organization of their paper.

Specific, technical feedback can also be helpful, but rather than correcting or editing the entire paper, faculty can share the types of technical issues the student will need to address. In addition, students can be encouraged to take advantage of support services such as tutoring. O'Neill and Gravois (2017) emphasized the importance of explaining why grammatically correct papers are so critical and training students on how to correct technical errors.

Formative Assessment Opportunities

Often, students may only have a few major assignments, and thus the opportunities for feedback are few and far between. Taras (2006) called on faculty to increase feedback opportunities for undergraduates, citing this as an equity issue where undergraduates are often treated unfairly. The argument is that undergraduate students who need feedback the most are the ones least likely to have opportunities to learn from feedback. Graduate students and faculty are often given revise-and-resubmit options, but undergraduate students typically do not have these opportunities. In most cases, undergraduates are given only summative assessments, major assignments that demonstrate whether they learned the knowledge and skills identified in the course learning outcomes. Summative assessments are typically high stakes, counting toward a large percentage of the final grade. Often, undergraduate students only have one chance at an exam, a paper, or a project, and although feedback will usually be provided, students do not often have the opportunity to use this feedback to improve their work.

One primary reason that undergraduates are often not given revise-and-resubmit options is because of time. Faculty teaching undergraduate courses have many more students than faculty teaching graduate courses, which means revise and resubmit opportunities come at a high cost of time for faculty. This makes incorporating formative assessments into courses a challenge. To increase feedback opportunities while considering the reality that there are only so many hours in a day, faculty may want to consider strategies such as using peer feedback and focused feedback and using class time to provide individual or small group feedback.

O'Neill and Gravois (2017) described how focused revision strategies can be used to help students improve their writing skills. One example is for faculty to build in revision opportunities very early on in the writing process when students are developing ideas for their paper. This approach involves asking students to identify at least two ideas for their paper. During class, students are given the opportunity to revise and strengthen their initial ideas and generate other possible areas of focus. This approach brings needed attention to the early phases of writing and the importance of examining ideas prior to jumping into the writing process. Another focused strategy that O'Neill and Gravois (2017) described is designed to help students revise grammatical errors. This approach involves training students on different types of grammatical errors and explaining why grammatical errors are problematic. Students are more likely to improve grammar when they see the benefits of doing so, and in this example students were able to see how producing papers free of grammatical errors would help their messages be better received by others. The revision activity was to keep a grammar log where they identified errors they made in their first draft and show the corrections made.

There are many approaches faculty can use to increase feedback opportunities. Incorporating numerous formative assessments into the course design is an excellent way to support student learning. Formative assignments are typically low stakes and provide meaningful feedback about progress toward learning. Feedback on formative assessments tells students whether they are on track to meet with success on the summative assignment and provides guidance on how to improve. When formative assessments are used, they usually count as only a small percentage of the final grade.

The following example by Jaclyn, a senior majoring in event management and hospitality, nicely illustrates how valuable formative assessments are to undergraduate students. She describes how getting feedback from her professor at various checkpoints during the semester enabled her and her group members to learn and improve.

Project Check-Ins
Jaclyn Bonacorda
Senior / Event Management and Hospitality Management
University of Central Florida
Course: Fine Spirits Management (midsized, hybrid class)

Our final project for the class was to create a bar with a creative theme and cocktail concept to fit that theme. Professor Orlowski had us hand in our project in phases so that she could give us feedback and help us to improve our work. This way, we would learn more and get a better grade on the final presentation. The first part of the project was to create our cocktail menu and then place each cocktail into the correct "family." Many cocktail families are very similar, and correctly categorizing each can be difficult. Even though my group had most of our cocktails in the wrong family, Professor Orlowski still gave us almost full credit on the check-in and later sat down with us to help us recategorize our menu. She went through our menu drink by drink and told us which cocktails were in the right or wrong family. She then worked with us to help us understand why the incorrect cocktails weren't correctly placed. Instead of telling us what the correct families were for each cocktail, she gave us the opportunity to correct what was wrong and then checked our project again to make sure we had every cocktail in the right family.

Professor Orlowski also encouraged us to come to her office hours at any time before our final project was due so that she could review our project and give us feedback to ensure we all did well on the final presentation. Her guidance made it easier to go back and review how we could improve our presentation. Rather than sitting around guessing, we were able to use the feedback provided to make changes to the presentation.

The way this project was set up made it clear that Professor Orlowski genuinely wanted us to learn the material, and this attitude made me more focused on learning and not just getting a good grade. I would encourage professors to build project "check-ins" into their grading scheme, as it is a good way for students to make sure they are on track with what the professor expects. Check-ins allow professors to provide constructive criticism to students to help them better understand the course material and help them to perform better. It also helps us to stay motivated and feel that the professor truly cares about how we do in the class.

Getting a subpar grade at the end of a large project with no chance to fix it would have been very discouraging. However, creating a final product we were proud of motivates us to keep learning.

⌘

As Jaclyn described, it can be very helpful to have a major summative project divided into smaller formative assessment opportunities. Students can then use the feedback they receive throughout the semester to improve so that they perform well on the final project. In the story that follows, Kayla, a graduate student, provides another example of how helpful it was to have a major project broken down into smaller assignments.

Breaking Down a Major Assignment
Kayla Jasper
Graduate student / Social Work / Temple University
Course: Evaluation of Clinical Practice (small, in-person class)

During my first semester of graduate school, I was required to take Evaluation of Clinical Practice. On paper, this class seemed daunting. As nervous as I was, I quickly realized how committed my professor was to helping us learn the material. In addition to the energy and positivity that she brought into class, our assignment schedule also helped put me at ease. We talked about the final project every week. Each class started with a lecture, followed by a hands-on activity, and ended with information regarding the final project due at the end of the semester.

My professor designed the final project to be completed throughout the semester by making pieces of it due on certain weeks leading up to the final date. This gave us the opportunity to complete the assignment one part at a time and receive feedback at each point. After the first assignment, she gave thorough feedback on what we could improve on for the next phase of the assignment. She made it clear that if we put in the effort, incorporated her comments and feedback, and followed the rubric that she provided, we would learn a lot and it would be difficult to earn a poor grade.

My professor also made herself available to students at any time. She encouraged us to reach out with questions and reassured us that she would answer emails in a timely manner. My class schedule did not allow me to go to her open office hours, but she made sure to stay late some days so that I received the same help as other students. My professor's commitment and passion for teaching this course were evident in the time and energy she gave to students. By providing feedback on assignments throughout the semester, I was able to gauge my understanding at several points throughout the course and focus on specific areas to improve.

Feedback is a crucial part of the learning process and necessary for students to understand the expectations set by professors for assignments. I would encourage other faculty to find ways to break down major assignments so students can see if they are on the right track and can seek out help if needed. This approach really helps us gain confidence and skills.

ᘜ

One challenge with feedback is that students often don't understand the feedback faculty provide. Only 55% of the students in a study conducted by Taylor (2011) reported understanding the reason for an instructor comment. When providing written feedback, typed feedback has been shown to be more effective than handwritten feedback. In a study conducted by Johnson et al. (2019), instructors provided more feedback, including more general observations, when sharing feedback in an electronic versus handwritten form, and students were more likely to improve when submitting revised work.

Providing feedback orally increases student understanding of feedback. This was illustrated in a study conducted by Voelkel and Mello (2014). Eighty-six percent of students who received audio feedback reported having no difficulty understanding the comments, while only 62% of students who received written feedback reported having no problem understanding the comments. Thus, audio comments were better understood. Those receiving audio feedback were also more satisfied with the level of detail and clarity, and several students commented that audio feedback was more personalized. Research conducted by Rawle et al. (2018) provides further support for the use of audio feedback. In this study, students reported that audio feedback was helpful and engaging because it was clear, constructive, detailed, and personalized. Despite the value of audio feedback, faculty may not want to rely on oral feedback exclusively. Students did note that it was easier to go back and review written versus audio feedback (Rawle et al., 2018).

In the next student story, Caleb describes how students were provided with both written and oral feedback throughout the semester and why this feedback led to increased engagement and learning.

Numerous Feedback Opportunities
Caleb E. Morris
Graduate student | Higher Education and Student Affairs
University of South Carolina
Course: Institutional Assessment in Higher Education (small, in-person class)

In her Institutional Assessment in Higher Education course, Professor Amber Fallucca engages students by providing frequent and constructive feedback on the assignments throughout the course. Professor Fallucca's use of frequent and constructive feedback made the assignments much more engaging and beneficial. For a semester-long client project, we had to complete an assessment planning worksheet, and her feedback on our plan was provided quickly and was very helpful. Students can potentially fall behind on project development or waste time going in the wrong direction if the feedback is not timely, relevant, and accurate. In addition to providing written feedback, Professor Fallucca also delivered oral, in-person feedback. At several points in the semester, Professor Fallucca devoted part of our class time, or sometimes a whole class period, to this major project. When she devoted a whole class period, she met with each group to get an update on the status of the project and provide feedback. The feedback provided was understandable, digestible, and thought-provoking, as Professor Fallucca framed it as a dialogue to help students learn how to improve the project and persist forward.

Professor Fallucca had students submit the course midterm assignment twice. After the first submission, she provided feedback and then asked students to revise and resubmit their work by a second deadline. Professor Fallucca posed guiding questions and referred students back to specific resources or readings that the students could use to strengthen their responses. This feedback and opportunity for revision was very helpful and added meaning to the assignment. Without it, students would probably not revisit the midterm and would, therefore, miss out on this learning opportunity. Having numerous opportunities to learn from the feedback was very helpful. I would encourage faculty to use a mix of written and oral feedback and to provide feedback often and in a timely fashion.

⚬⚭⚬

Some faculty may opt to grade formative assessments, but this isn't always necessary. Students in a study conducted by Lipnevich and Smith (2009) noted that grades were not needed when the goal was learning. Some students even noted that not receiving a grade enabled them to really focus on the comments and improving their work. This results in increased learning and better grades.

In the following example, Annie, a doctoral student, shares how feedback without a grade was incredibly empowering and engaging for her.

Ungraded Assignments
Annie Kelly
Graduate student who is employed full time I Curriculum and Instruction
Loyola University Chicago
Course: Educational Evaluation (small, in-person class)

During the first year of my doctoral program, I took Educational Evaluation, which was a program evaluation class taught by Professor Leanne Kallemeyn. This class was an extraordinary learning experience as it was the first time I had submitted assignments that were not for a grade and were intentionally rooted in practical application. Professor Kallemeyn structured the curriculum so that six assignments were submitted throughout the semester as components of a cumulative program evaluation project. The assignments were nongraded and returned with constructive and reflective formative feedback I could use to better understand the scholarship and practice of program evaluation, assess my own learning over time, and apply her feedback to strengthen my final project, which was for a grade.

Peer review was also embedded, and we frequently took class time to constructively critique each other's work. Another engaging element was that an experiential learning opportunity was integrated into every assignment. For example, one of the assignments was to submit a program description with evaluation questions, which had to be intentionally coconstructed with the program's stakeholders. This allowed me the opportunity to translate my program evaluation knowledge into practical application and receive timely, formative feedback on how to best engage with stakeholders. The six assignments were further complemented by readings, case studies, and the American Evaluation Association's guiding principles that informed our study and application. When it was time to submit the cumulative project, I believe I created a project that was nicely aligned with the guiding principles of program evaluation.

There were four key elements that made the assignment engaging. First, it was nongraded and designed to help the learner grow. This was the first time I experienced an assignment where I felt highly motivated to learn and engage with the material because I knew I could make mistakes and take risks without consequence. Second, the assignment was socially constructed in both how we collaborated with program stakeholders and during peer review. Peer review allowed me the opportunity to both communicate and receive diverse feedback and perspectives on my project. Third, Professor Kallemeyn allowed us to choose the program we would evaluate. Choice and ownership of the material were critical to my engagement, especially as I was able to select a program aligned with my dissertation research interests. Fourth, the assignment was experiential and integrative. I was able to apply the knowledge, understanding, and skills of program evaluation directly to a project. This experience, coupled with the assigned readings and case studies, allowed me to further integrate my learning to create new meaning and understanding of program evaluation. These interconnected elements created an environment that motivated and encouraged me to take ownership and engage in my learning.

While this assignment structure can be an empowering learning experience, Professor Kallemeyn shared that some students can become anxious over how the final project will be graded. She combatted this by having one graded assignment at the beginning of the semester where students had to find and analyze a program evaluation report. This assists students in understanding how she grades and gives feedback. While acknowledging this limitation, there are many benefits to implementing this assignment structure. Through using nongraded feedback, peer review, student choice, and experiential and integrative learning opportunities, educators can maximize student learning, motivation, and engagement within assignments. As a result of this learning experience, I have been able to deeply understand and apply the principles of program evaluation.

Incorporating Peer Feedback Opportunities

Peer feedback has many advantages. Smith (2012) identified several benefits of an online peer review system, including that it increases transparency, capitalizes on social learning, highlights the value of peers as resources, and improves the overall learning experience for all. However, many students struggle with how to give valuable feedback, especially if they lack confidence in their ability to successfully complete the task. Asking students to provide peer feedback without giving them structure and support will not likely work out well.

In the following student story, Elena, a sophomore, explains how her professor used class time for the peer review process and why this engaged her as a learner.

Peer Review Sessions
Elena St. Amour
Sophomore | Psychology and Chemistry | Drew University
Course: Drew Seminar: Hogwarts, Houses, and Horcruxes: The Psychology of Harry Potter (small, in-person class)

To keep the class engaged and to help us perform our best, the professor of this course had peer review sessions in class where peers with similar essay topics would get together and discuss how the writing process of the essay has been going and exchange papers to receive feedback on what had been written so far. There was also a writing fellow in the class who previously took and passed the course. In addition to providing help during class, the writing fellow also made time outside the class for students to come ask questions and receive feedback.

This was incredibly useful because we would get tons of feedback on our papers from classmates who were writing on similar topics, a writing fellow who had taken the course previously, and the professor. All this feedback was provided well before the due date. By receiving feedback from peers, I learned how to make my essay flow better so that someone who had no idea what my topic was about would understand my writing. The professor walked around the room and gave feedback on individual essays, asked about how the writing process was going for each student, read the drafts of our papers, and made suggestions for improvement. This assistance helped me strengthen my papers and kept me engaged. I enjoyed seeing the work of my peers and getting feedback on my work.

For other teachers and professors who would want to engage their students this way, they could schedule days throughout the semester dedicated to peer editing and learning new writing strategies so that students are less overwhelmed by essays. As a first-year student in this course, having those writing days removed most of the stress of essays and even made them more enjoyable to write. Professors can encourage peers to interact with each other about their writing and even possibly have someone who had previously taken and done well in the course be available to provide feedback and answer questions. Having that kind of person around, as well as having encouragement to interact with peers, provided a way to receive help without feeling intimidated by the professor.

Peer feedback processes can add value to both in-person and online courses. In the following example, Robert, an online graduate student, describes how his professor incorporated several layers of peer feedback into an assignment. This approach helped him feel connected to his classmates and helped him grow as an online learner.

Layers of Peer Feedback
Robert J. Portella
Graduate student who is a working professional / Adult and Continuing Education
Rutgers University
Course: Organizational Leadership (small, online class)

The offering of peer feedback is a truly powerful mechanism that can be used in several different ways to help students think critically about their work, reflect on their assignments, and consider multiple perspectives. I have been fortunate to have had opportunities to learn from my peers through the peer feedback process. In this course, the professor spent time setting up the structure for how the peer review would work. First, we had to write a statement of purpose or a small paragraph so that our peers would be able to gain just a little insight into our goal for the assignment. Next, we were instructed to ask one another Socratic questions. Finally, we had to formally review each other's project.

The Socratic questions helped us consider all the different angles of our project. For example, my peers asked me to consider the assumptions behind the statements I made and challenged me to consider other viewpoints. In addition, peers asked me to consider the implications of what I was proposing, which forced me to think forward about the potential and impact of my ideas. Finally, my peers also asked me what someone who disagreed would say, and this forced me to consider the direct opposite approach, thereby enabling me to construct richer thoughts that directly addressed any opposition.

When it came time for peers to review drafts, I was initially afraid to submit my work for fear of too much critique; however, my professors cited the necessity of pointing out both negatives and positives in the assignment. I feel this is important; the feedback naturally encourages me to be satisfied with a job well done but also allows me to step back and critically consider what my peers had suggested to improve my work. Often, no two pieces of feedback were similar, so this meant I had to personally evaluate the feedback and make meaning out of the reviews. The suggestions provided caused me to pause and reflect on the work I had done and determine if the suggested changes would help me improve my final product.

The feedback was provided in several different ways. We had asynchronous opportunities via discussion posts where peers could offer thoughts at their leisure. Then, we had a window of time to submit VoiceThread comments vocally. Finally, when we were in small groups or pairs, we had the opportunity to either chat online or speak on the phone with each other to have even more personalized conversations about the feedback.

When I work on an assignment of any kind, I get so invested that I lose sight of ways to improve or evolve my own work. Having the benefits of peer review broadens my own vision of the current work and gives me ideas to tuck away for future work. I believe it is tremendously beneficial for the professors to let the students review one another's work as often as possible in a draft state—or, depending on the class learning outcomes, even the final submission—so that the person generating the work can reap the rewards of multiple perspectives. Providing a structure can help students give meaningful feedback.

ॐ

Grades are one way to communicate the importance of peer review. Thus, faculty may want to consider grading the feedback students provide to their peers. Students will then be more likely to provide high-quality feedback to their peers, increasing the likelihood that peer feedback adds value to the learning process. If feedback is graded, it can be helpful to provide students with guidelines about what is expected.

In the following student story, Sarah shares how a graded peer feedback experience helped her grow as a learner.

Graded Peer Feedback

Sarah Lyman Kravits
Returning adult, online graduate student, mother of three, who is employed
Education / Rutgers University, New Brunswick
Course: Introduction to Teaching With Digital Tools (small, online class)

The capstone assignment for this course required students to apply everything that we had learned in the course up until that point to design a website. The assignment was situated effectively in the course calendar, far enough into the semester that we could apply a wide range of relevant learning to the experience of completing the assignment, but with enough time left in the course for the students to comment on one another's websites and learn from exploring one another's work. One of the requirements of the assignment was to provide feedback to at least two peers. The required feedback also had a point value in the total grade for the assignment.

The invitation to review all the websites created, and the requirement to provide feedback on at least two of them, extended our learning. From exploring other students' sites, I learned about other digital tools I had not implemented, saw new uses for ones I had implemented, experienced unique and creative ways of putting a site together and designing the user experience, and learned from the students' descriptions of the goals they were intending to accomplish with their sites. From the feedback on my own website, I received thoughtful ideas about how I could continue to improve my work and modify it for different goals or audiences.

For faculty who want to utilize peer feedback with this type of capstone assignment, I would suggest situating the assignment due late in the course but with enough time for students to review one another's work and learn from it. Additionally, I highly recommend attaching a point value to peer feedback. Having

the feedback be a graded portion of the capstone assignment and providing dead-
lines both increase the likelihood that students will do what they are asked to do
and benefit from it.

❧

As illustrated in the student stories, peer feedback can be extremely helpful.
It provides students with helpful suggestions and different perspectives. Having
the opportunity to see the work of classmates is also a learning experience as it
exposes students to different approaches and content. However, it is important
to note that peer feedback is not always valuable. Achen (2018) found that peer
feedback was the least preferred type of feedback by students. Students cited
several reasons for not valuing peer feedback, including peers not fully understanding the expectations of the assignment, lack of expertise, and peers providing comments that are nice but not helpful. Providing structure and training
to students before asking them to provide feedback to one another can increase
the likelihood that the peer review process is a productive one.

Facey (2011) shares strategies to increase the quality of peer feedback.
For example, a peer conveyor-belt model approach that requires students
to provide feedback on only one aspect of the project is recommended.
The instructor begins by identifying approximately three to four aspects
of the project. Students are then assigned to a group and provided with a
brief training on how to give feedback on their assigned aspect or part of
the assignment. One group might focus on citations only, another might
be looking for main ideas, and so forth. During class, student papers then
cycle through each group, hence the conveyor-belt title. Students review the
paper, providing feedback on only their assigned aspect or part. By the time
the paper gets back to the person who wrote it, there should be feedback on
all of the aspects. Students feel more competent giving this type of targeted
feedback and find the comments provided by peers more useful since
everyone had a specific focus.

Peer feedback is often most helpful when it is more objective than subjective. For example, instead of asking students to provide overall feedback
on a peer's paper, Nilson (2003) suggests asking students specific questions
about the paper that require no judgment or expertise. For example, students
could be asked to make an outline of the paper. This can help students see
the organizational structure and flow of the paper through the eyes of a peer.
Students may also be asked to underline or star what they believe is the major
or primary point of each paragraph and indicate how many supporting ideas
were provided. Students can also be asked to put a notation near sentences or
paragraphs that were not clear to them.

Giving Students Opportunities to Revise

Research shows that students value the opportunity to revise and will do so for minimal incentives (Garner & Shank, 2018). Students report that opportunities to submit a draft and to rewrite papers are very helpful (Achen, 2018). It is important for faculty to help students see revision as a part of the process. Successful people constantly engage in the revision process, and this results in higher-quality work.

In the student story that follows, Kara shares how her professor helped her see the value of revising her work and how proud she was of the final artwork. She notes how these experiences were especially important to her as a member of marginalized and underrepresented groups.

Pushing Me to Improve
Kara Infelise
Returning adult sophomore / Graphic Communications
Gateway Technical College
Course: Illustration Media and Computer Illustration (small, in-person class)

Clear, fair, and concise feedback and grading can help make or break the drive to succeed for a student, especially a student who has dealt with hardships throughout life because of skin color, gender, or sexual orientation, such as myself. Society already tells people of color that we can only achieve so much success. Fighting those stereotypes at every turn in life can be exhausting, so to have a professor who truly believes in students and wants to see them succeed and do well in life can give those fighting a silent struggle that final push they need to keep going.

Professor Laznicka has been an incredible driving force for me to keep going through life's struggles. She pushed me to be better. By always giving me constructive feedback on the work I've done and telling me that she knows I am capable, she has inspired me to revise and improve my work. She never let me be anything less than amazing because that's what she saw in me. Her door was always open should there be questions or confusion, or if I simply needed someone to lean on. This has been a huge key to my success and drive to continue my education.

Feedback that is constructive and helps me see how to improve is what I need. Even something as simple as, "This part was great; now let's work on this part. Come see me after class and let's go over some options" drives me to keep working at it. I remember one time during my illustration class, I presented a pen-and-ink drawing. Professor Laznicka knew I already put in a lot of work into this project but also knew that I was capable of something better. She sat down with me and talked to me about adjusting the layout. For example, she suggested moving this tree here, making things smaller, and using better types of trees for the scenery. I went back and started the entire drawing over again, but the finished product is something I'm very proud of—a product I wouldn't have created if my professor had not taken just a few moments out of her day to sit down with me and critique my work.

If we see that our teachers care, truly care, then we will care more about what we're doing and the quality of the work we produce. And that's especially true for minorities. We need our teachers to care about us and our opinions. We're so underrepresented in society that our voices get lost in the crowd. But if our professors help us build the confidence we need to succeed by investing in us as human beings, that will stay with us forever.

༷

As Kara shared, feedback plays a critical role in success. Receiving feedback is an emotional process. It takes courage for students to share drafts and work products with their peers and professors. Feedback that inspires and encourages is important to all learners, but, as Kara pointed out, it is especially important to students from marginalized or underrepresented groups. Giving students an opportunity to revise and resubmit their work communicates your belief in them. Feltham and Sharen (2015) found that students significantly improved when given the opportunity to submit revised work. Thus, these opportunities can build self-efficacy and skills.

Many factors, such as confidence, emotions, and professor–student relationships, play a role in how students perceive and use feedback. For example, Pitt and Norton (2017) found that confidence can impact how feedback is interpreted and that feedback received can increase or decrease a student's confidence. Feedback is emotional, and because of this many students have self-defensive reactions that prevent them from using the feedback to improve (Forsythe & Johnson, 2017). Students acknowledge that it can be difficult to hear feedback. They appreciate and value feedback that is concise; constructive in nature; and shared in a sensitive, supportive, personal, and encouraging way (Lowe & Shaw, 2019).

Students often have negative reactions to poor grades, especially if suggestions on how to improve are not provided (Lipnevich & Smith, 2009). Forsythe and Johnson (2017) recommended that faculty prepare students early in the semester for feedback, emphasizing the goal of feedback. In addition, they recommended that faculty infuse opportunities to discuss feedback with students so that they can provide personalized assistance to students, showing them how to use feedback for improvement.

Faculty can foster a growth mindset in their students through the feedback process. Many students have a fixed mindset, and this gets in the way of them using feedback to improve (Forsythe & Johnson, 2017). Students who can revise their work are more likely to have a growth mindset (Feltman & Sharen, 2015). Thus, the experience of being able to improve work through revision helped students see that effort plays a significant role in their success, and this belief will lead to them exerting higher levels of effort in the future.

In the following student example, Amy, a doctoral student, talks openly about how feedback is emotional. She describes how a revision opportunity enabled her to shift from feeling like a failure to gaining confidence with research skills.

Building Skills Through Revision Opportunities
Amy Hankins
Graduate student who is a working professional / Community College Leadership
New Jersey City University
Course: The Scholarly Practitioner (small, online class)

I was in the first year of my doctorate program, and I had a lengthy annotation assignment to complete. I figured I could do it—no problem. I was mistaken. It was more difficult than I had imagined to locate literature I needed, and, once I had the studies, I found it very challenging to write brief annotations on complex studies. This was a new experience for me, and I felt like I was failing. After spending a significant amount of time on this project, I turned it in, crossing my fingers and my stomach hurting.

Thankfully, I quickly got a response from my instructor. However, it was not what I was hoping for, which was an A on the assignment. Instead, there was no grade and a request to revise it. Though I was "almost there" with the assignment goals, I had missed the mark on several elements. I had been too brief on some; missed recording part of a study's results in another; and in others, I had been too loquacious. My professor gave me written feedback, which I used as a step-by-step guide to revise my work.

Although the revision process was incredibly time-consuming, I surprisingly went from feeling like a failure to being motivated and buoyed! In addition to carefully reviewing the feedback from the professor and having conversations with her about how to improve, I also turned to my peers who had excelled on this assignment and ask them for suggestions, feedback, and examples of how they did their assignments. With more time and different types of effort, I was successful.

Ultimately, I will never forget the feeling of trying as hard as I could but still feeling like I was in the dark to feeling like I was on my way to mastering a new skill. The suggestions by my professor and peers helped me improve my knowledge and skills. This experience also allowed me more compassion as an instructor myself. I have been much more aware of giving my students second chances when needed, not to mention building time into the semester for revisions. This experience helped me remember what it was like to be a student who was struggling and feeling like a failure. The opportunity to have a few more days to revise was a saving grace and an important reminder of how challenging the process of learning can be.

ॐ

Brief educational interventions can help students shift from a fixed mindset to a growth mindset, and this results in many positive outcomes.

For example, Smith et al.'s (2018) research showed that faculty actions before feedback situations arise can have a positive impact. In this experimental study, Smith et al. (2018) discovered that when an instructor used growth mindset language ("Everyone can learn statistics if they try") prior to a lesson, it resulted in increased growth mindset beliefs and higher performance on tests.

Feedback that emphasizes a growth mindset makes a difference. In an experimental study conducted by Bostwick and Becker-Blease (2018), students were randomly assigned to one of three groups: growth mindset, fixed mindset, or control group. After taking a pretest, students received feedback based on their assigned group. The feedback for the growth mindset group emphasized how the brain can learn skills and adapt and that they could overcome obstacles by working hard and adapting. The fixed mindset group of students received feedback that emphasized how everyone has strengths and weaknesses and that those who are successful learn how to use their strengths. The control group feedback talked about how attending class is important and thanked them for being a great student.

Results indicated that students in the growth mindset group had higher midterm exam and final exam scores compared to students in the fixed mindset group and control group. These findings indicate that brief, easy-to-implement feedback can help students achieve at higher levels. To help students develop a growth mindset, Dweck (2008) suggests that educators praise the process or efforts made by students who are successful. When students miss the mark, faculty can provide constructive feedback that focuses on factors in students' control such as trying a different strategy or approach. The key is for students to walk away believing they can improve and do better if they do more or engage in different actions.

In the following example, Erin shares how a second chance motivated her to do well and how it helped her grow and develop.

Second Chance
Erin Stern
Graduate student / Occupational Therapy / Worcester State University
Courses: Organizational and Professional Issues 1, Thesis Seminar 1, Thesis Seminar 2, Thesis Seminar 3 (small, in-person classes)

In this course sequence, we had to write a 50-plus page thesis that incorporated research we had done along with a self-created survey and study materials. My professor helped us by breaking down the workload into multiple different parts or check-in points to ensure progress. This made an overwhelming task less daunting. Many of these assignments had two versions. An initial version was written and submitted for grading. If the written assignment received full credit, there was no need for the second version. However, if there were some mistakes in the first version, the professor noted where improvements could be made. Then, we were responsible for going back and submitting those corrections for grading again.

It was nice knowing that if I didn't meet the expectations I didn't have to panic. I would have a second chance. The professor's suggestions and comments on the original piece really fostered my learning and pinpointed my areas of weakness and things to work on without directly giving me the answer. Although I knew the professor was available to help, this approach allowed me to learn and problem-solve on my own. Faculty who use this second chance for grading can motivate students to do well the first time but discover that mistakes are not the end of the world. We all discovered that we could grow and improve and that our professor was there to support us.

Ⓧ

When giving students the opportunity to revise and resubmit, faculty may want to consider adding a reflective essay component to the final submission. This can encourage students to think deeply about the feedback they received. In an interesting study conducted by Ducasse and Hill (2019), students were required to reflect on their learning by reviewing feedback received and explaining whether they used the feedback and, if so, how. Results indicated that students found this experience valuable. Specifically, 84% of the student participants reported that they took more responsibility for their learning. Students commented that they used feedback more than they did in the past to improve their work.

In the following student story, Ryan describes how a reflection and question activity related to the feedback he received engaged him as a learner and led to an improved product.

Required Revisions
Ryan Harrington
Senior | Marketing | Quinnipiac University
Course: Marketing Channels and Distribution (small, in-person class)

In this course, one of the major assignments was a group project that included a presentation and a paper. About halfway through the semester, the paper portion of this project was due. The professor graded the papers by the following class, and when he returned the papers to each group he explained how we would be spending the entire class reviewing our papers. The professor then spoke to the whole class describing the requirements of this revision assignment. He told us that we would be receiving a separate grade for this second, revised submission. Knowing that this assignment was going to be graded again, we immediately became more interested in the notes and feedback that the professor had written on the returned papers. The professor then went to each group and spent 5 to 10 minutes discussing that group's paper with the group members while the other groups were working on the presentation portion of the project.

When providing feedback to the group, he went through the paper page by page and explained where the paper could be improved and what the group did well. An important note here is that the feedback he wrote on the physical paper was not extremely detailed but highlighted the key issues with the paper. This created a scenario where the discussion he had with the groups was extremely important, and the students would need to ask a plethora of quality questions in order to properly understand what was expected of the group. The conversation was extremely valuable. It's not typical to get to discuss feedback about a paper with your professor.

The professor required us to ask him several questions about his feedback so that he could guarantee there was no confusion about what we needed to do. At first, many of us didn't understand why the professor was requiring us to ask questions about his feedback and the paper, but after the first question or two, we recognized the benefit of asking questions about the feedback. Rather than the professor simply reiterating what he wrote on the paper, the questions led to an extremely productive conversation about the paper and the feedback. This was an unusual but welcome learning experience.

Having the opportunity to revise our work for a grade motivated us to carefully review and consider the feedback provided to us. It motivated us to ask genuine questions because there was an incentive to have a productive conversation focused on how to improve our work. This method of providing feedback proved to be very effective at getting us to investigate and understand the feedback that the professor provided us. During my personal collegiate career, this was the best experience I've had with professor feedback. It was a useful tool that helped me learn. I strongly encourage other faculty to have conversations with their students about their work and to require students to ask questions about the feedback.

❧

Ryan's story highlights the value of face-to-face feedback. This can be time-consuming, but the example just shared shows how a professor was able to utilize class time for this purpose. Research shows the benefit of this approach. Although there were no statistically significant differences on the final product submitted by students who received written feedback only and students who received written feedback and had a conference with the instructor, Isnawati et al. (2019) noted a higher level of engagement for students who participated in the meeting with the instructor as evidenced by asking more questions. When students are more engaged, they are more likely to learn.

Providing Feedback to High-Achieving Students

Often, conversations about feedback are focused on assisting students who are struggling with tasks. In these situations, feedback plays a critical role in helping students be successful. However, it is also important that all students get to benefit from feedback, even students who may already be doing very well. Even if a student has demonstrated that they achieved the learning outcome, they can still improve skills.

Many high-achieving students receive minimal feedback, and this is often in the form of praise. Sometimes, high-achieving students may only receive a grade and not any comments at all. When comments are provided, they are often generic in nature. Students in a study conducted by Lipnevich and Smith (2009) who received a high grade without any comments were happy but did not engage in any reflection or revision. It is important for faculty to challenge and support all students, and although struggling students may need more feedback and support, high-achieving students can also be challenged to improve.

In the following student story, Kayla, a community college student, shares how one of her professors acknowledged her high level of achievement yet still challenged her in several ways.

Supporting Me as an "A" Student
Kayla Wathen
Sophomore | Biology | Middlesex County College
Course: Genetics (small, in-person class)

It is very common for professors to provide feedback and insight to students who tend to struggle more in the class or seem to need more of a push to be motivated. However, it is far less common for professors to take notice of students who are high achieving and tend to go above and beyond in the classroom. As a student who strives to achieve the best grades and put maximum effort into every class, I have noticed that sometimes it is easy for our work to go unnoticed.

Ever since I started at Middlesex County College, I have always put 100% of my effort into my classes because getting a solid foundation of knowledge in the curriculum and achieving good grades is my top priority. Sometimes I would just get a pat on the shoulder, but this was not the case with Professor Gardner. She had the perfect balance of providing help to struggling students as well as making sure the work of excelling students did not go unnoticed. As a student who took her classes very seriously and strove for nothing lower than an "A," I can say with confidence that her tactics made me feel very proud of all the hard work I put into each class. For example, she always commented about the value I added to class discussions and listened to my concerns and took them into consideration. Recognizing that I wanted to be challenged, Professor Gardner invited me to be a teaching assistant for her general biology lab and to assist her with her personal research. Having opportunities like this could benefit me in a multitude of ways in the future, and it was so nice to be recognized for the hard work I put into the classes.

Even when I earned an "A" on an assignment, Professor Gardner would always provide feedback to me, highlighting my strong areas but also pointing out areas where I could improve. She challenged me to submit my very best work by encouraging me and helping me strengthen some weaker areas. One comment that she would often say really stuck with me. She said that we should always submit our best work and act as if the person who will be grading it has no idea who we are. In other words, the work would be the only way for the person reading it to get to know what kind of student we are.

Overall, I know that some students need more support than others. It is important, though, for professors to recognize high-achieving students and make sure that their hard work does not go unnoticed. We want to be challenged, too. Help us reach our highest potential. These are just some of the many ways that professors can make their high-achieving students feel recognized, proud of their hard work, and inspired to do even better.

☙❧

In the next student example, Michael, a senior, explains how helpful it was for his professor to know his goals and to push him to excel. Although Michael is an "A" student, this course was outside of his comfort zone. He describes how his professor's actions really made a difference for him.

Pushing Me to Excel
Michael Daidone
Senior / Chemistry / College of the Holy Cross
Course: Philosophy of Literature (small, in-person class)

On the first day of class, my professor handed us a syllabus that outlined a semester filled with unfamiliar novels and stories. My stomach sank, knowing I had my work cut out for me. The professor divided the class into four sections, corresponding to four novels, and required an essay at the completion of each. As an experienced and savvy student, I began reading and preparing ideas for the essay well ahead of the assigned due date. I prepared the first draft, made edits to my essay over the course of a few days, and submitted the paper well before the deadline. However, despite these efforts, I received a B on the paper. I worked hard again, submitted the second paper, and again received a B. Although some students might be satisfied with this grade, this grade was far off the standard I had set for myself. Halfway through my first semester of senior year in Philosophy of Literature, I knew the grades I received weren't of concern, never in jeopardy of failing the class, or even close to a C; however, I was not satisfied.

Most students who receive a paper back marked with the words "come see me" feel a sense of doom, that they've submitted something so appalling it warrants discipline, but those words, marked in red pen on the top of the second philosophy paper are exactly what saved my semester in this course. I had previously met with the professor at the beginning of the semester, letting him know I was out of my comfort zone, being one of the only chemistry majors in this upper-level philosophy class. Thus, he knew my expectations of what I was hoping to get out of the class, what kind of student I was, and what kind of grade I was hoping to achieve. After receiving two "B's" on my first two papers, he wanted to discuss my progress to help me improve and reach my goals. Although the three dreaded words "come see me" were concerning at first, I really appreciated how much my professor knew me and was willing to help. Many professors would not encourage students who are doing well in a course to come and see them, but this one knew that I was capable of more and that I had high aspirations. For a professor to recognize a "B" as a poor grade in the mind of some students is uncommon on a college campus; however, it's all relative to the student.

After this conversation, I excelled in this class, not merely because of the feedback I received, but because I knew my professor cared about me in this intricate sort of way and that was motivating. To many students, grades are the end all be all, and a professor may view this attitude as unproductive or even the antithesis of education. However, students do need to learn more in order to achieve high grades. When this professor reached out to me about my current standing, despite it being a very respectable score, I better understood the goals of each essay and discovered ways I could improve. Because of this meeting, I had a more motivated mindset that resulted in me stretching myself. Knowing the support and care my professor had for me inspired me to think more deeply about the novels and produce higher-quality essays.

I would encourage all faculty to get to know your students and their aspirations and goals for your class. Provide students, even high-achieving students, with constructive criticism, guidance, and support. Too often, we are given minimal feedback and not pushed to excel.

∞

Providing positive feedback can help students see their potential and can motivate them to seek out learning opportunities. In some cases, students may not see their strengths as clearly as professors do. In these situations, it can be quite empowering for students to receive positive feedback and encouragement from their professors. In other cases, students may be aware of their strengths, but having a professor bring attention to these strengths can be validating and motivating. In the following student story, Christina shares how her professor acknowledged her strengths and helped her develop the confidence to seek out more challenging learning opportunities.

Reinforcing Strengths
Christina Christodoulou
Senior | Psychology | Drew University
Course: Social Psychology (small, in-person class)

Although it is important that students discover how they need to improve, it is just as critical for students to understand their strengths and for these strengths to be reinforced and further developed. I have always considered myself a strong technical writer, which, as a psychology major, has been one of my greatest assets. However, it wasn't until my social psychology professor left a very positive comment on one of my papers regarding my writing style that I began to feel truly confident both in my writing and in my future in the field of psychology.

For one of our assignments, we had to write an advertising campaign to encourage healthy eating. As I was designing my campaign, I realized that I was truly enjoying the assignment and genuinely becoming passionate about the topics of both social psychology and marketing. Even so, I found this paper, as well as several similar assignments, to be extremely challenging and unlike any project I had completed before. Therefore, I felt very unsure of my work as I submitted the assignment.

When I received my graded paper and reviewed my professor's comments, I became more confident about my knowledge and skills. My professor noted some areas in which my project could have been improved, providing several thoughtful and insightful suggestions. Knowing that my professor had taken ample time to provide thorough comments inspired me to continue to improve as a writer and critical thinker. At the same time, he noted various strengths that I displayed throughout my project. This really boosted my confidence in my abilities. He even commented that I demonstrated many qualities of a professional in the area of social psychology and that he could see me having a successful career in the field. Knowing that my professor truly believed in me and my potential as a technical writer, psychological thinker, and fulfilled academic was really motivating.

This positive feedback gave me the confidence I needed to seek out other learning opportunities. For example, I applied to and participated in my college's New York City semester on media and communications where I expanded my horizons as a journalistic writer and developed an in-depth understanding of careers in the fields of communications and social psychology. I also worked at my university's tutoring center as a scientific writing specialist, where I continued to enhance my skills as a writer, an editor, and a creative thinker in the area of psychology. The constructive and inspiring grading approaches of my social psychology professor and many others have enabled me to push myself to a higher standard each time I submit a paper and have also given me the confidence to apply to various psychology graduate programs.

Students are more likely to be engaged and feel motivated to improve in areas in which they feel that their professor believes in their potential and is invested in their growth. Many students have skills, but they may not realize their potential and may lack the confidence necessary to develop their strengths and evolve in their fields. For professors to engage their students through their feedback and grading approaches, it is vital that they identify and reinforce academic assets in order to increase students' positivity toward their own work. Moreover, it is especially crucial for professors to provide constructive criticism as well as note areas of strength when students are tasked with an assignment that challenges them and leaves them unsure of themselves. Such positive feedback is likely to increase their confidence and facilitate motivation.

かわ

Faculty who believe in their students are more likely to provide feedback that challenges and supports. In other words, if a faculty member believes in a student's potential, they are more likely to push, challenge, and guide a student. In contrast, if a faculty member does not believe in a student, they will probably not push and challenge them. In an interesting study by Harber et al. (2012), faculty were asked to give feedback to students. Each essay had demographic information about each student, including race and ethnicity. The results revealed significant differences in the type of feedback given based on race and ethnicity. Specifically, it was found that White public school teachers gave more positive feedback to students of color versus White students. The authors noted that the lack of challenging feedback for students of color likely contributes to underachievement. Supportive feedback can sometimes be helpful, but it doesn't typically result in increased learning.

It is important for faculty to be aware of biases and perceptions that can influence the type of feedback we provide. Malouff et al. (2014) conducted an experimental study on the halo effect that showed bias based on prior performance. Students who performed well on a prior assignment were given higher grades compared to students who did not perform as well despite the assignment being the same.

Because of bias in grading, faculty may want to consider grading assignments blindly, without names attached (Malouff et al., 2014). One approach that is being used on some campuses is computerized feedback. Although students were at first hesitant to receive computerized feedback versus personalized feedback from an instructor, some students shared how they believed this method was less biased (Lipnevich & Smith, 2009). Anonymous or computerized grading may not always be possible or desirable. Feldman (2020) made the following suggestions to make grading more equitable: Use a 0–4 versus 0–100 scale, grade knowledge versus effort, give students an opportunity to revise work and use the revised grade in final grade calculation, and provide guidelines such as rubrics to help students know what is expected.

Faculty Reflection Questions

1. How can I increase formative assessment opportunities so that students can immediately apply feedback to improve their work?
2. When might it be appropriate to provide feedback without grades?
3. How can I use peer feedback to improve student learning? What type of training and support will students need to provide valuable feedback? How can I incorporate this part of the process into the assignment grade?

4. When can I give my students opportunities to revise and resubmit work?
5. When students revise their work, how can I ensure that they gain maximum value from this process?
6. How can I promote a growth mindset through the type of feedback that I provide?
7. What type of support can I provide to struggling and high-achieving students?
8. How can I reduce the influence of bias when grading assignments and providing feedback?

Achen, R. M. (2018). Addressing the "my students cannot write" dilemma: Investigating methods for improving graduate student writing. *Journal of the Scholarship of Teaching and Learning, 18*(4), 71–85. https://doi.org/10.14434/josotl.v18i4.23040

Alexandrin, J. R., French, J. J., & DeLeon, W. (2008). Diversity education at a predominately White Catholic college. *Multicultural Perspectives, 10*(2), 94–99. https://doi.org/10.1080/15210960801997973

Aloni, M., & Harrington, C. (2018). Research-based practices for improving the effectiveness of asynchronous online discussion boards. *Scholarship of Teaching and Learning in Psychology, 4*(4), 271–289. https://doi.org/10.1037/stl0000121

Ascend & Institute for Women's Policy Research. (2019). *Parents in college: By the numbers.* Aspen Institute. https://ascend.aspeninstitute.org/wp-content/uploads/2019/04/2019-Parents-in-College_By-the-Numbers-Ascend_IWPR.pdf

Bailey, S., Barber, L. K., & Ferguson, A. J. (2015). Promoting perceived benefits of group projects: The role of instructor contributions and intragroup processes. *Teaching of Psychology, 42*(2), 179–183. https://doi.org/10.1177/0098628315573147

Baker, L. R., & Hitchcock, L. I. (2017). Using Pinterest in undergraduate social work education: Assignment development and pilot survey results. *Journal of Social Work Education, 53*(3), 535–545. https://doi.org/10.1080/10437797.2016.1272515

Baker, S. (2012). Classroom karaoke. *Youth Studies Australia, 31*(1), 25–33.

Bandura, A., & Walters, R. H. (1963). *Social learning and personality development.* Holt, Rinehart & Winston.

Bartolomeo-Maida, M. (2016). The use of learning journals to foster textbook reading in the community college psychology class. *College Student Journal, 50*(3), 440–453.

Beattie, I. R., & Thiele, M. (2016). Connecting in class? College class size and inequality in academic social capital. *Journal of Higher Education, 87*(3), 332–362. https://doi.org/10.1080/00221546.2016.11777405

Berry, T., Cook, L., Hill, N., & Stevens, K. (2011). An exploratory analysis of textbook usage and study habits: Misperceptions and barriers to success. *College Teaching, 59*(1), 31–39. https://doi.org/10.1080/87567555.2010.509376

Bombardieri, M. (2019, September 25). How to fix education's racial inequities, one tweak at a time. *Politico.* https://www.politico.com/agenda/story/2019/09/25/higher-educations-racial-inequities-000978

Bostwick, K. C. P., & Becker-Blease, K. A. (2018). Quick, easy mindset intervention can boost academic achievement in large introductory psychology classes. *Psychology Learning and Teaching, 17*(2), 177–193. https://doi.org/10.1177%2F1475725718766426

Bowen, J. (2012). *Teaching naked: How moving technology out of your college classroom will improve student learning.* Jossey-Bass.

Brank, E., & Wylie, L. (2013). Let's discuss: Teaching students about discussions. *Journal of the Scholarship of Teaching and Learning, 13*(3), 23–32. https://files.eric.ed.gov/fulltext/EJ1017045.pdf

Brookfield, S. D. (2015). *The skillful teacher: On technique, trust, and responsiveness in the classroom* (3rd edition). Jossey-Bass.

Brown, S. (2015). Authentic assessment: Using assessment to help students learn. *Electronic Journal of Educational Research, Assessment & Evaluation, 21*(2), 1–8.

Cameron, M. P. (2012). "Economics with training wheels": Using blogs in teaching and assessing introductory economics. *Journal of Economic Education, 43*(4), 397–407. https://doi.org/10.1080/00220485.2012.714316

Campus Compact (n.d.). *Service-learning.* https://compact.org/initiatives/service-learning/

Carver, C. S. (1998). Resilience and thriving: Issues, models, and linkages. *Journal of Social Issues, 54*(2), 245–266. https://doi.org/10.1111/0022-4537.641998064

Case, K. F. (2013). Teaching strengths, attitudes, and behaviors of professors that contribute to the learning of African-American and Latino/a college students. *Journal on Excellence in College Teaching, 24*(2), 129–154.

Caspersz, D., & Olaru, D. (2017). The value of service-learning: The student perspective. *Studies in Higher Education, 42*(4), 685–700. https://doi.org/10.1080/03075079.2015.1070818

Cate, R., & Russ-Eft, D. (2018). A review of current methods to develop empowering service learning programs for Latina/o college students. *Journal of Hispanic Higher Education, 17*(3), 216–228. https://doi.org/10.1177%2F1538192717729735

Caulfield, S. L., & Persell, C. H. (2006). Teaching social science reasoning and quantitative literacy: The role of collaborative groups. *Teaching Sociology, 34*(1), 39–53. https://doi.org/10.1177/0092055X0603400104

Cavanagh, S. R. (2019, March 11). How to make your teaching more engaging. *The Chronicle of Higher Education.* https://www.chronicle.com/interactives/advice-teaching

Cell Press. (2006, August 27). Pure novelty spurs the brain. *ScienceDaily.* https://www.sciencedaily.com/releases/2006/08/060826180547.htm

Center for Community College Student Engagement. (2009). *Making connections: Dimensions of student engagement (2009 CCSSE findings).* The University of Texas at Austin, Community College Leadership Program. https://www.ccsse.org/publications/national_report_2009/CCSSE09_nationalreport.pdf

Center for Community College Student Engagement. (2010). *The heart of student success: Teaching, learning, and college completion (2010 CCCSE findings).*

The University of Texas at Austin, Community College Leadership Program. https://cccse.org/sites/default/files/2010_National_Report.pdf

Center for Community College Student Engagement. (2015). *Engagement rising: A decade of CCSSE data shows improvements across the board.* The University of Texas at Austin, Program in Higher Education Leadership. https://cccse.org/sites/default/files/Engagement_Rising.pdf

Chan, M. (2019). An analysis of new student orientation programs at U.S. four-year colleges: How can administrators enhance the first and major milestone of a student's academic journey? *Planning for Higher Education Journal, 47*(3), 38–52.

Chan, S. C., Ngai, G., & Kwan, K. (2019). Mandatory service learning at university: Do less inclined students learn from it? *Active Learning in Higher Education, 20*(3), 189–202. https://doi.org/10.1177%2F1469787417742019

Chávez, A. F., & Longerbeam, S. D. (2016). *Teaching across cultural strengths: A guided to balancing integrated and individuated cultural frameworks in college teaching.* Stylus.

Cheng, P., & Cheou, W. (2010). Achievement, attributions, self-efficacy, and goal setting by accounting undergraduates. *Psychological Reports, 106*(1), 54–64. https://doi.org/10.2466/pr0.106.1.54-64

Chickering, A. W., & Gamson, Z. F. (1987). Seven principles for good practice in undergraduate education. *AAHE Bulletin, 39*(7), 3–7. http://www.aahea.org/articles/sevenprinciples1987.htm

Chiriac, E. H. (2014). Group work as an incentive for learning—students' experiences of group work. *Frontiers in Psychology, 5*, 1–10. https://dx.doi.org/10.3389%2Ffpsyg.2014.00558

Colbeck, C. L., Campbell, S. E., & Bjorklund, S. A. (2000). Grouping in the dark: What college students learn from group projects. *Journal of Higher Education, 71*(1), 60–83. http://dx.doi.org/10.2307/2649282

Connelly, R. (2014, February 24). *Reflecting on the handshake problem.* National Council of Teachers of Mathematics. https://www.nctm.org/Publications/Teaching-Children-Mathematics/Blog/Reflecting-on-the-Handshake-Problem/

Cook, B. R., & Babon, A. (2017). Active learning through online quizzes: Better learning and less (busy) work. *Journal of Geography in Higher Education, 41*(1), 24–38. https://doi.org/10.1080/03098265.2016.1185772

Cooper, K. S., & Miness, A. (2014). The co-creation of caring student-teacher relationships: Does teacher understanding matter? *High School Journal, 97*(4), 264–290. http://doi.org/10.1353/hsj.2014.0005

Crist, C. (2018, November 1). Mental health diagnosis rising among U.S. college students. *Reuters.* https://www.reuters.com/article/us-health-mental-college/mental-health-diagnoses-rising-among-u-s-college-students-idUSKCN1N65U8

Croes, J., & Visser, M. M. (2015). From tech skills to life skills: Google online marketing challenge and experiential learning. *Journal of Information Systems Education, 26*(4), 305–316. https://pdfs.semanticscholar.org/ee17/16db3b1d0a093b1c1b3d90f317ed79ea620b.pdf?_ga=2.244198401.568619763.1596746364-1947270477.1596746364

Crosby, O. (2010). Informational interviewing: Get the inside scoop on careers. *Occupational Outlook Quarterly, 54*(2), 22–29. https://www.bls.gov/careerout look/2010/summer/art03.pdf

Cundell, A., & Sheepy, E. (2018). Student perceptions of the most effective and engaging online learning activities in a blended graduate seminar. *Online Learning, 22*(3), 87–102. http://dx.doi.org/10.24059/olj.v22i3.1467

Cuseo, J. (2018). Student-faculty engagement. *New Directions for Teaching & Learning, 2018*(154), 87–97. https://doi.org/10.1002/tl.20294

Daluba, N. E. (2013). Effect of demonstration method of teaching on students' achievement in agricultural science. *World Journal of Education, 3*(6), 1–7. https://doi.org/10.5430/wje.v3n6p1

Davis, L., & Fry, R. (2019, July 31). *College faculty have become more racially and ethnically diverse, but remain far less so than students.* Pew Research Center. https://www.pewresearch.org/fact-tank/2019/07/31/us-college-faculty-student-diversity/

Dawson, M., & Pooley, J. A. (2013). Resilience: The role of optimism, perceived parental autonomy support and perceived social support in first year university students. *Journal of Education and Training Studies, 1*(2), 38–49. https://doi.org/10.11114/jets.v1i2.137

Delfino, A. P. (2019). Student engagement and academic performance of students of Partido State University. *Asian Journal of University Education, 15*(1), 1–16. https://files.eric.ed.gov/fulltext/EJ1222588.pdf

Demir, M., Burton, S., & Dunbar, N. (2018). Professor-student rapport and perceived autonomy support as predictors of course and student outcomes. *Teaching of Psychology, 46*(1), 22–33. https://doi.org/10.1177%2F0098628318816132

Dickinson, A. (2017). Communicating with the online student: The impact of e-mail tone on student performance and teacher evaluations. *Journal of Educators Online, 14*(2), 1–11. https://doi.org/10.9743/jeo.2017.14.2.5

Dixon, J. S., Crooks, H., & Henry, K. (2006). Breaking the ice: Supporting collaboration and the development of community online. *Canadian Journal of Learning and Technology, 32*(2), 1–20. https://doi.org/10.19173/irrodl.v8i2.444

Drago, A., Rheinheimer, D. C., & Detweiler, T. N. (2018). Effects of locus of control, academic self-efficacy, and tutoring on academic performance. *Journal of College Student Retention: Research, Theory & Practice, 19*(4), 433–451. https://doi.org/10.1177/1521025116645602

Ducasse, A. M., & Hill, K. (2019). Developing student feedback literacy using educational technology and the reflective feedback conversation. *Practitioner Research in Higher Education, 12*(1), 24–37. https://files.eric.ed.gov/fulltext/EJ1212986.pdf

Durham, F. D., Russell, J.-E., & Van Horne, S. (2018). Assessing student engagement: A collaborative curriculum for large lecture discussion sections. *Journalism and Mass Communication Educator, 73*(2), 218–236. https://doi.org/10.1177/1077695817713431

Dweck, C. S. (2008). Mindsets: How praise is harming youth and what can be done about it. *School Library Monthly, 24*(5), 55–58. http://www.cs4all.org/files/1831922.pdf

Eccles, J. S., & Wigfield, A. (2002). Motivational beliefs, values, and goals. *Annual Review of Psychology, 53*(1), 109–132. https://doi.org/10.1146/annurev.psych.53.100901.135153

Ennen, N., Stark, E. E., & Lassiter, A. (2015). The importance of trust for satisfaction, motivation, and academic performance in student learning groups. *Social Psychology of Education, 18*(3), 615–633. https://doi.org/10.1007/s11218-015-9306-x

Espino-Bravo, C. (2015, October 27). *U*sing personal stories to engage students in conversation. *Faculty Focus.* https://www.facultyfocus.com/articles/teaching-and-learning/using-personal-stories-to-engage-students-in-conversation/

Facey, J. (2011). "A is for assessment" . . . strategies for A-level marking to motivate and enable students of all abilities to progress. *Teaching History, 144,* 36–43.

Feldman, J. (2020, January 27). Improved grading makes classrooms more equitable. *Inside Higher Ed.* https://www.insidehighered.com/views/2020/01/27/advice-how-make-grading-more-equitable-opinion

Feltham, M., & Sharen, C. (2015). "What do you mean I wrote a C paper?" Writing, revision, and self-regulation. *Collected Essays on Learning and Teaching, 8*(2015), 111–138. https://files.eric.ed.gov/fulltext/EJ1069881.pdf

Finney, S., & Pyke, J. (2008). Content relevance in case-study teaching: The alumni connection and its effect on student motivation. *Journal of Education for Business, 83*(5), 251–257. https://doi.org/10.3200/JOEB.83.5.251-258

Fleck, B., Hussey, H. D., & Rutledge-Ellison, L. (2017). Linking class and community: An investigation of service learning. *Teaching of Psychology, 44*(3), 232–239. https://doi.org/10.1177/0098628317711317

Forsythe, A., & Johnson, S. (2017). Thanks, but no-thanks for the feedback. *Assessment & Evaluation in Higher Education, 42*(6), 850–859. https://doi.org/10.1080/02602938.2016.1202190

Friedman, J. (2017, April 4). U.S. News data: The average online bachelor's student. *U.S. News & World Report.* https://www.usnews.com/higher-education/online-education/articles/2017-04-04/us-news-data-the-average-online-bachelors-student

Garner, B., & Shank, N. (2018). Student perceptions of a revise and resubmit policy for writing assignments. *Business & Professional Communication Quarterly, 81*(3), 351–367. https://doi.org/10.1177/2329490618784962

Garrison, D. R., Anderson, T., & Archer, W. (2000). Critical inquiry in a text-based environment: Computer conferencing in higher education. *The Internet and Higher Education, 2*(2–3), 87–105. https://doi.org/10.1016/S1096-7516(00)00016-6

Gehlbach, H., Brinkworth, M. E., King, A. M., Hsu, L. M., McIntyre, J., & Rogers, T. (2016). Creating birds of similar feathers: Leveraging similarity to improve teacher-student relationships and academic achievement. *Journal of Educational Psychology, 108*(3), 342–352. https://doi.org/10.1037/edu0000042

Goldberg, N. A., & Ingram, K. W. (2011). Improving student engagement in a lower-division botany course. *Journal of the Scholarship of Teaching and Learning, 11*(2), 76–90. https://files.eric.ed.gov/fulltext/EJ932147.pdf

Greenbank, P., & Hepworth, S. (2008). *Working class students and the career decision-making process: A qualitative study.* HECSU. http://www.hecsu.ac.uk/assets/assets/documents/Working_class.pdf

Griffin, C. P., & Howard, S. (2017). Restructuring the college classroom: A critical reflection on the use of collaborative strategies to target student engagement in higher education. *Psychology Learning and Teaching, 16*(3), 375–392. https://doi .org/10.1177/1475725717692681

Gubera, C., & Aruguete, M. S. (2013). A comparison of collaborative and traditional instruction in higher education. *Social Psychology of Education, 16*(4), 651–659. https://doi.org/10.1007/s11218-013-9225-7

Harber, K. D., Gorman, J. L., Gengaro, F. P., Butisingh, S., Tsang, W., & Ouellette, R. (2012). Students' race and teachers' social support affect the positive feedback bias in public schools. *Journal of Educational Psychology, 104*(4), 1149–1161. https://doi.org/10.1037/a0028110

Harnish, R. J., & Bridges, K. (2011). Effect of syllabus tone: Students' perceptions of instructor and course. *Social Psychology of Education: An International Journal, 14*(3), 319–330. https://doi.org/10.1007/s11218-011-9152-4

Harrington, C., & Gabert-Quillen, C. (2015). Syllabus length and use of images: An empirical investigation of student perceptions. *Scholarship of Teaching and Learning in Psychology, 1*(3), 235–243. https://doi.org/10.1037/stl0000040

Harrington, C., & Thomas, M. (2018). *Designing a motivational syllabus: Creating a learning path for student engagement.* Stylus.

Harrington, C., & Zakrajsek, T. (2017). *Dynamic lecturing: Research-based strategies to enhance lecture effectiveness.* Stylus.

Harris, G., & Bristow, D. (2016). The role of group regulation in student groups: A pedagogical exploration. *e-Journal of Business Education & Scholarship of Teaching, 10*(2), 47–59. https://files.eric.ed.gov/fulltext/EJ1167319.pdf

Hollins, T. N. (2009). Examining the impact of a comprehensive approach to student orientation. *The Journal of Virginia Community Colleges, 14*(1), 15–27. https://files.eric.ed.gov/fulltext/EJ833916.pdf

Hrepic, Z., Zollman, D., & Rebello, S. (2004). Students' understanding and perceptions of the content of a lecture. *AIP Conference Proceedings, 720*(1), 189–192. https://doi.org/10.1063/1.1807286

Hulleman, C. S., Kosovich, J. J., Barron, K. E., & Daniel, D. B. (2017). Making connections: Replicating and extending the utility value intervention in the classroom. *Journal of Educational Psychology, 109*(3), 387–404. https://doi.org/ 10.1037/edu0000146

Ismail, N., & Sabapathy, C. (2016). Workplace simulation: An integrated approach to training university students in professional communication. *Business and Professional Communication Quarterly, 79*(4), 487–510. https://doi.org/10.1177/ 2329490616660814

Isnawati, I., Sulistyo, G. H., Widiati, U., & Suryati, N. (2019). Impacts of teacher-written corrective feedback with teacher-student conference on students' revision. *International Journal of Instruction, 12*(1), 669–684. https://doi.org/10.29333/ iji.2019.12143a

Johnson, W. F., Stellmack, M. A., & Barthel, A. L. (2019). Format of instructor feedback on student writing assignments affects feedback quality and student performance. *Teaching of Psychology*, *46*(1), 16–21. https://doi.org/10.1177/0098628318816131

Joyce, H. D. (2015). School connectedness and student-teacher relationships: A comparison of sexual minority youths and their peers. *Children & Schools*, *37*(3), 185–192. https://doi.org/10.1093/cs/cdv012

Jozwiak, J. (2015). Helping students to succeed in general education political science courses? Online assignments and in-class activities. *International Journal of Teaching and Learning in Higher Education*, *27*(3), 393–406. https://files.eric.ed.gov/fulltext/EJ1093759.pdf

Karpova, E., Jacobs, B., Lee, J. Y., & Andrew, A. (2011). Preparing students for careers in the global apparel industry: Experiential learning in a virtual multi-national team-based collaborative project. *Clothing & Textiles Research Journal*, *29*(4), 298–313. https://doi.org/10.1177/0887302X11421809

Kim, Y. (2015). Learning statics through in-class demonstration, assignment and evaluation. *International Journal of Mechanical Engineering Education*, *43*(1), 23–37. https://doi.org/10.1177/0306419015574643

Knowles, M. S., Holton, E. F., & Swanson, R. A. (2012). *The adult learner: The definitive classic in adult education and human resource development* (7th edition). Routledge.

Komarraju, M., & Nadler, D. (2013). Self-efficacy and academic achievement: Why do implicit beliefs, goals, and effort regulation matter? *Learning and Individual Differences*, *25*, 67–72. https://doi.org/10.1016/j.lindif.2013.01.005

Kuh, G. D., Kinzie, J., Cruce, T., Shoup, R., & Gonyea, R. M. (2007). *Connecting the dots: Multi-faceted analyses of the relationships between student engagement. Results from the NSSE, and the institutional practices and conditions that foster success*. Center for Postsecondary Research, Indiana University Bloomington. https://scholarworks.iu.edu/dspace/bitstream/handle/2022/23684/Connecting%20the%20dots-%20Multi-faceted%20analyses%20of%20the%20relationships%20between%20student%20engagement%20results%20from%20the%20NSSE,%20and%20the%20institutional%20practices%20and%20conditions%20that%20foster%20student%20success.pdf

Kurpis, L. H., & Hunter, J. (2017). Developing students' cultural intelligence through an experiential learning activity: A cross-cultural consumer behavior interview. *Journal of Marketing Education*, *39*(1), 30–46. https://doi.org/10.1177/0273475316653337

Landrum, R. E., Gurung, R. R., & Spann, N. (2012). Assessments of textbook usage and the relationship to student course performance. *College Teaching*, *60*(1), 17–24. https://doi.org/10.1080/87567555.2011.609573

Lang, J. M. (2019, January 4). How to teach a good first day of class advice guide. *The Chronicle of Higher Education*. https://www.chronicle.com/interactives/advice-firstday

Laws, E. L., Apperson, J. M., Buchert, S., & Bregman, N. J. (2010). Student evaluations of instruction: When are enduring first impressions formed? *North American Journal of Psychology*, *12*(1), 81–92.

Lei, H., Cui, Y., & Zhou, W. (2018). Relationships between student engagement and academic achievement: A meta-analysis. *Social Behavior & Personality: An International Journal, 46*(3), 517–528. https://doi.org/10.2224/sbp.7054

Lightner, R., & Benander, R. (2018). First impressions: Student and faculty feedback on four styles of syllabi. *International Journal of Teaching & Learning in Higher Education, 30*(3), 443–453. https://files.eric.ed.gov/fulltext/EJ1199421.pdf

Linksz, D. (1990). *Faculty inventory: Seven principles for good practices in undergraduate education.* Catonsville Community College, Office of Institutional Research. https://files.eric.ed.gov/fulltext/ED316276.pdf

Lipnevich, A., & Smith, J. (2009). "I really need feedback to learn:" Students' perspectives on the effectiveness of the differential feedback messages. *Educational Assessment, Evaluation & Accountability, 21*(4), 347–367. https://doi.org/10.1007/s11092-009-9082-2

Locke, E. A., & Latham, G. P. (2002). Building a practically useful theory of goal setting and task motivation: A 35-year odyssey. *American Psychologist, 57*(9), 705–717. https://doi.org/10.1037/0003-066X.57.9.705

Lowe, T., & Shaw, C. (2019). Student perceptions of the "best" feedback practices: An evaluation of student-led teaching award nominations at a higher education institution. *Teaching & Learning Inquiry, 7*(2), 121–135. https://doi.org/10.20343/teachlearninqu.7.2.8

Lucardie, D. (2014). The impact of fun and enjoyment on adult's learning. *Procedia Social and Behavioral Sciences, 142*(2014), 439–446. https://doi.org/10.1016/j.sbspro.2014.07.696

Lundberg, C. A. (2014). Peers and faculty as predictors of learning for community college students. *Community College Review, 42*(2), 79–98. https://doi.org/10.1177/0091552113517931

Malouff, J. M., Stein, S. J., Bothma, L. N., Coulter, K., & Emmerton, A. J. (2014). Preventing halo bias in grading the work of university students, *Cogent Psychology, 1*, 1–9. https://doi.org/10.1080/23311908.2014.988937

Manzano-Sanchez, H., Outley, C., Gonzalez, J. E., & Matarrita-Cascante, D. (2018). The influence of self-efficacy beliefs in the academic performance of Latina/o students in the United States: A systematic literature review. *Hispanic Journal of Behavioral Sciences, 40*(2), 176–209. https://doi.org/10.1177/0739986318761323

Marriott, P., Tan, S. M., & Marriott, N. (2015). Experiential learning: A case study of the use of computerized stock market trading simulation in finance education. *Accounting Education, 24*(6), 480–497. https://doi.org/10.1080/09639284.2015.1072728

Martin, F., & Bolliger, D. U. (2018). Engagement matters: Student perceptions on the importance of engagement strategies in the online learning environment. *Online Learning, 22*(1), 205–222. https://doi.org/10.24059/olj.v22i1.1092

Mather, M., & Sarkans, A. (2018). Student perceptions of online and face-to-face learning. *International Journal of Curriculum and Instruction, 10*(2), 61–76. http://ijci.wcci-international.org/index.php/IJCI/article/view/178/72

McClenney, K., Mari, C. N., & Adkins, C. (2007). *Student engagement and student outcomes: Key findings from CCSSE validation research.* Community College Leadership Program at The University of Texas at Austin. https://cccse.org/sites/default/files/CCSSE_Validation_Summary.pdf

McClenney, K. M. (2007). Research update: The Community College Survey of Student Engagement. *Community College Review, 35*(2), 137–146. https://doi.org/10.1177/0091552107306583

McGinley, J. J., & Jones, B. D. (2014). A brief instructional intervention to increase students' motivation on the first day of class. *Teaching of Psychology, 41*(2), 158–162. https://doi.org/10.1177/0098628314530350

McGuire, G. M. (2000). Gender, race, ethnicity, and networks: The factors affecting the status of employees' network members. *Work and Occupations, 27*(4), 500–523. https://doi.org/10.1177/0730888400027004004

Micari, M., & Pazos, P. (2012). Connecting to the professor: Impact of the student-faculty relationship in a highly challenging course. *College Teaching, 60*(2), 41–47. https://doi.org/10.1080/87567555.2011.627576

Miller, A. L. (2018). The role of creative coursework in skill development for university seniors. *Global Education Review, 5*(1), 88–107. https://files.eric.ed.gov/fulltext/EJ1177632.pdf

Miller, S. T., & Redman, S. L. (2010). Enhancing student performance in an online introductory astronomy course with video demonstrations. *Astronomy Education Review, 9*(1), 1–10. https://doi.org/10.3847/AER2009066

Millis, B. (2014). Using cooperative structures to promote deep learning. *Journal on Excellence in College Teaching, 25*(3–4), 139–148. http://www.jufsusanne.nl/files/uploads/deep-learning-artikelen/v25n34-millis.pdf

Milne, C., & Otieno, T. (2007). Understanding engagement: Science demonstrations and emotional energy. *Science Education, 91*(4), 523–553. https://doi.org/10.1002/sce.20203

Muddiman, A., & Frymier, A. B. (2009). What is relevant? Student perceptions of relevance strategies in college classrooms. *Communication Studies, 60*(2), 130–146. https://doi.org/10.1080/10510970902834866

Mushi, S. L. P. (2001). *Teaching and learning strategies that promote access, equity, and excellence in university education.* Author. https://files.eric.ed.gov/fulltext/ED449760.pdf

National Center for Education Statistics. (2020, April). *Characteristics of postsecondary students.* https://nces.ed.gov/programs/coe/indicator_csb.asp

National Survey of Student Engagement. (2013). *A fresh look at student engagement: Annual results 2013.* https://scholarworks.iu.edu/dspace/bitstream/handle/2022/23406/NSSE_2013_Annual_Results.pdf

Ngai, G., Chan, S. C. F., & Kwan, K. (2018). Challenge, meaning, interest, and preparation: Critical success factors influencing student learning outcomes from service-learning. *Journal of Higher Education Outreach and Engagement, 22*(4), 55–80. https://files.eric.ed.gov/fulltext/EJ1202022.pdf

Nicol, D. J., & Macfarlane-Dick, D. (2006). Formative assessment and self-regulated learning: A model and seven principles of good feedback practice. *Studies in Higher Education, 31*(2), 199–218. https://doi.org/10.1080/03075070600 572090

Nilson, L. B. (2003). Improving student peer feedback. *College Teaching, 51*(1), 34–38. https://doi.org/10.1080/87567550309596408

Nilson, L. B. (2016). *Teaching at its best: A research-based resource for college instructors* (4th edition). Jossey-Bass.

O'Neill, K. S., & Gravois, R. (2017). Using a focus on revision to improve students' writing skills. *Journal of Instructional Pedagogies, 19*, 1–12. https://files.eric.ed.gov/fulltext/EJ1158379.pdf

Ozan, C. (2019). Authentic assessment increased academic achievement and attitude towards the educational measurement of prospective teachers. *International Journal of Evaluation and Research in Education, 8*(2), 299–312. http://doi.org/10.11591/ijere.v8i2.18564

Padron, T. C., Fortune, M. F., Spielman, M., & Tjoei, S. (2017). The job shadow assignment: Career perceptions in hospitality, recreation and tourism. *Research in Higher Education Journal, 32*, 1–20. https://files.eric.ed.gov/fulltext/EJ1148919.pdf

Parker, L. L., & Loudon, G. M. (2013). Case study using online homework in undergraduate organic chemistry: Results and student attitudes. *Journal of Chemical Education, 90*(1), 37–44. https://doi.org/10.1021/ed300270t

Patchan, M. M., Schunn, C. D., & Correnti, R. J. (2016). The nature of feedback: How peer feedback features affect students' implementation rate and quality of revisions. *Journal of Educational Psychology, 108*(8), 1098–1120. https://doi.org/10.1037/edu0000103

Patel, S. (2016, March 9). Why feeling uncomfortable is the key to success. *Forbes.* https://www.forbes.com/sites/sujanpatel/2016/03/09/why-feeling-uncomfortable-is-the-key-to-success

Payne, B. K., Monk-Turner, E., Smith, D., & Sumter, M. (2006). Improving group work: Voices of students. *Education, 126*(3), 441–448. https://digitalcommons.odu.edu/cgi/viewcontent.cgi?article=1023&context=sociology_criminaljustice_fac_pubs

Peng, J., & Abdullah, I. (2018). Building a market simulation to teach business process analysis: Effects of realism on engaged learning. *Accounting Education, 27*(2), 208–222. https://doi.org/10.1080/09639284.2017.1407248

Perna, L. W. (2010). *Understanding the working college student.* American Association of University Professors. https://www.aaup.org/article/understanding-working-college-student#.XY1uf0ZKjD4

Phillips, F., & Wolcott, S. (2014). Effects of interspersed versus summary feedback on the quality of students' case report revisions. *Accounting Education, 23*(2), 174–190. https://doi.org/10.1080/09639284.2013.847328

Pitt, E., & Norton, L. (2017). "Now that's the feedback I want!" Students' reactions to feedback on graded work and what they do with it. *Assessment & Evaluation in Higher Education, 42*(4), 499–516. https://doi.org/10.1080/02602938.2016.1142500

Prichard, J. S., Stratford, R. J., & Bizo, L. A. (2006). Team-skills training enhances collaborative learning. *Learning and Instruction, 16*(3), 256–265. https://doi.org/10.1016/j.learninstruc.2006.03.005

Priniski, S. J., Hecht, C. A., & Harackiewicz, J. M. (2018). Making learning personally meaningful: A new framework for relevance research. *Journal of Experimental Education, 86*(1), 11–29. https://doi.org/10.1080/00220973.2017.1380589

Rabourn, K. E., BrckaLorenz, A., & Shoup, R. (2018). Reimagining student engagement: How nontraditional adult learners engage in traditional postsecondary environments. *The Journal of Continuing Higher Education, 66*(1), 22–33. https://doi.org/10.1080/07377363.2018.1415635

Rakow, L. (1991). Gender and race in the classroom: Teaching way out of line. *Feminist Teacher, 6*(1), 10–13.

Rawle, F., Thuna, M., Zhao, T., & Kaler, M. (2018). Audio feedback: Student and teaching assistant perspectives on an alternative mode of feedback for written assignments. *Canadian Journal for the Scholarship of Teaching and Learning, 9*(2), 1–21. https://doi.org/10.5206/cjsotl-rcacea.2018.2.2

Redding, C. (2019). A teacher like me: A review of the effect of student-teacher racial/ethnic matching on teacher perceptions of students and student academic and behavioral outcomes. *Review of Educational Research, 89*(4), 499–535. https://doi.org/10.3102/0034654319853545

Robinson, D. (2019). Engaging students on the first day of class: Student-generated questions promote positive course expectations. *Scholarship of Teaching and Learning in Psychology, 5*(3), 183–188. https://doi.org/10.1037/stl0000139

Rodriguez, R. J., & Koubek, E. (2019). Unpacking high-impact instructional practices and student engagement in a teacher preparation program. *International Journal for the Scholarship of Teaching & Learning, 13*(3), 1–9. https://doi.org/10.20429/ijsotl.2019.130311

Roehling, P. V., Vander Kooi, T. L., Dykema, S., Quisenberry, B., & Vandlen, C. (2011). Engaging the millennial generation in class discussions. *College Teaching, 59*(1), 1–6. https://doi.org/10.1080/87567555.2010.484035

Rogmans, T., & Abaza, W. (2019). The impact of international business strategy simulation games on student engagement. *Simulation & Gaming, 50*(3), 393–407. https://doi.org/10.1177/1046878119848138

Rose, T. M. (2018). Lessons learned using a demonstration in a large classroom of pharmacy students. *American Journal of Pharmaceutical Education, 82*(9), 1081–1085. https://doi.org/10.5688/ajpe6413

Sarfo, F., & Elen, J. (2011). Investigating the impact of positive resource interdependence and individual accountability on students' academic performance in cooperative learning. *Electronic Journal of Research in Educational Psychology, 9*(1), 73–93. https://doi.org/10.25115/ejrep.v9i23.1428

Seider, S., Huguley, J. P., & Novick, S. (2013). College students, diversity, and community service learning. *Teachers College Record, 115*, 1–40. https://pdfs.semanticscholar.org/3287/0fb03fb07456c3ba659e746209e22d348878.pdf

Sever, S., Oguz-Unver, A., & Yurumezoglu, K. (2013). The effective presentation of inquiry-based classroom experiments using teaching strategies that employ video and demonstration methods. *Australasian Journal of Educational Technology, 29*(3), 450–463. https://doi.org/10.14742/ajet.229

Sheer, V. C., & Fung, T. K. (2007). Can email communication enhance professor-student relationship and student evaluation of professor?: Some empirical evidence. *Journal of Educational Computing Research, 37*(3), 289–306. https://doi.org/10.2190/EC.37.3.d

Shin, R. (2011). Social justice and informal learning: Breaking the social comfort zone and facilitating positive ethnic interaction. *Studies in Art Education, 53*(1), 71–87. https://doi.org/10.1080/00393541.2011.11518853

Smith, M. (2012). Can online peer review assignments replace essays in third year university courses? And if so, what are the challenges? *Electronic Journal of E-Learning, 10*(1), 147–158. https://files.eric.ed.gov/fulltext/EJ969452.pdf

Smith, T., Brumskill, R., Johnson, A., & Zimmer, T. (2018). The impact of teacher language on students' mindsets and statistics performance. *Social Psychology of Education, 21*(4), 775–786. https://doi.org/10.1007/s11218-018-9444-z

Steingut, R. R., Patall, E. A., & Trimble, S. S. (2017). The effect of rationale provision on motivation and performance outcomes: A meta-analysis. *Motivation Science, 3*(1), 19–50. https://doi.org/10.1037/mot0000039

Stern, L. A., & Solomon, A. (2006). Effective faculty feedback: The road less traveled. *Assessing Writing, 11*(1), 22–41. https://doi.org/10.1016/j.asw.2005.12.001

Supiano, B. (2020, February 6). To improve persistence this college asks professors to have a 15-minute meeting with each student. *The Chronicle of Higher Education*. https://www.chronicle.com/article/To-Improve-Persistence-This/247986

Swanson, E., McCulley, L. V., Osman, D. J., Scammacca Lewis, N., & Solis, M. (2019). The effect of team-based learning on content knowledge: A meta-analysis. *Active Learning in Higher Education, 20*(1), 39–50. https://doi.org/10.1177/1469787417731201

Sweeney, A., Weaven, S., & Herington, C. (2008). Multicultural influences on group learning: A qualitative higher education study. *Assessment & Evaluation in Higher Education, 33*(2), 119–132. https://doi.org/10.1080/02602930601125665

Taras, M. (2006). Do unto others or not: Equity in feedback for undergraduates. *Assessment & Evaluation in Higher Education, 31*(3), 365–377. https://doi.org/10.1080/02602930500353038

Taylor, S. S. (2011). "I really don't know what he meant by that": How well do engineering students understand teachers' comments on their writing? *Technical Communication Quarterly, 20*(2), 139–166. https://doi.org/10.1080/10572252.2011.548762

Terrenzini, P. (2011). *Past and prologue: Thoughts on 30 years of the Annual Conference on the First-Year Experience*. Paper presented at the 30th Annual Conference of the First-Year Experience, Atlanta, GA.

Tews, M. J., Jackson, K., Ramsay, C., & Michel, J. W. (2015). Fun in the college classroom: Examining its nature and relationship with student engagement. *College Teaching, 63*(1), 16–26. https://doi.org/10.1080/87567555.2014.972318

Tropman, E. (2014). In defense of reading quizzes. *International Journal of Teaching and Learning in Higher Education, 26*(1), 140–146. https://files.eric.ed.gov/fulltext/EJ1043037.pdf

Van Hoye, G., van Hooft, E. A. J., & Lievens, F. (2009). Networking as a job search behavior: A social network perspective. *Journal of Occupational and Organizational Psychology, 82*(3), 661–682. https://doi.org/10.1348/096317908X360675

Vilorio, D. (2011). Focused job seeking: A measured approach for looking for work. *Occupational Outlook Quarterly, 55*(1), 2–11. https://www.bls.gov/careeroutlook/2011/spring/art01.pdf

Voelkel, S., & Mello, L. V. (2014). Audio feedback—better feedback? *Bioscience Education Electronic Journal, 22*(1), 16–30. https://doi.org/10.11120/beej.2014.00022

Wang, L., & Calvano, L. (2018). Understanding how service learning pedagogy impacts student learning objectives. *Journal of Education for Business, 93*(5), 204–212. https://doi.org/10.1080/08832323.2018.1444574

Wigfield, A., & Eccles, J. S. (2000). Expectancy-value theory of achievement motivation. *Contemporary Educational Psychology, 25*(1), 68–81. https://doi.org/10.1006/ceps.1999.1015

Wilson, J. H., Ryan, R. G., & Pugh, J. L. (2010). Professor-student rapport scale predicts student outcomes. *Teaching of Psychology, 37*(4), 246–251. https://doi.org/10.1080/00986283.2010.510976

Wlodkowski, R. J. (2008). *Enhancing adult motivation to learn: A comprehensive guide for teaching all adults.* Jossey-Bass.

Wollschleger, J. (2019). Making it count: Using real-world projects for course assignments. *Teaching Sociology, 47*(4), 314–324. https://doi.org/10.1177/0092055X19864422

Wu, Z. (2019). Academic motivation, engagement, and achievement among college students. *College Student Journal, 53*(1), 99–112.

Christine Harrington is a national expert in student success and teaching and learning. Harrington earned her BA in psychology and MA in counseling and personnel services from The College of New Jersey and her PhD in counseling psychology from Lehigh University. She has worked in higher education for over 20 years. Currently, she is an associate professor and a coordinator of a newly established EdD in community college leadership program at New Jersey City University. She also teaches part-time in the Learning and Teaching Department within the Graduate School of Education at Rutgers University. Previously, she worked at Middlesex County College for 18 years in a variety of roles including professor of psychology and student success, director for the Center for the Enrichment of Learning and Teaching, first-year seminar course coordinator, counselor, and disability services provider. Harrington also served a 2-year appointment as the executive director for the Center for Student Success at the New Jersey Council of County Colleges.

Harrington is the author of numerous books and articles related to teaching and learning. She coauthored *Dynamic Lecturing: Research-Based Strategies to Enhance Lecture Effectiveness* with Todd Zakrajsek (Stylus, 2017), *Designing a Motivational Syllabus: Creating a Learning Path for Student Engagement* with Melissa Thomas (Stylus, 2018), and *Why the First-Year Seminar Matters: Helping Students Choose a Career Path* with Theresa Orosz (Rowman and Littlefield, 2018). She authored *Engaging Faculty in Guided Pathways: A Practical Resource for College Leaders* (Rowman and Littlefield and the American Association of Community Colleges, 2020) and *Ensuring Learning: Supporting Faculty to Improve Student Success* (Rowman and Littlefield and the American Association of Community Colleges, 2020). She also authored a research-based first-year seminar textbook titled *Student Success in College: Doing What Works! 3rd edition* (Cengage, 2019). She was the 2016 recipient of the Excellence in Teaching First-Year Experience award which was presented at the Annual Conference on the First-Year Experience, and the recipient of the 2016 Middlesex County College Faculty Excellence in Teaching Award. She is frequently invited to give plenary presentations at national and local conferences as well as at colleges and universities across the nation.

academic achievement, 1, 2, 22, 35, 43, 75
academic performance, 43, 46, 47, 69, 72, 86, 102
Achen, 118–119
adult learner, 3
advising, 50, 51, 56
Alexandrin, 97
Aloni, 73
anti-Semitic, 63–64, 97
anxiety, 1, 84
ascend, 46
assignments, 15, 17–18, 24–25, 27–33, 38–39, 42–43, 45–49, 54–55, 57, 62–66, 70–71, 74, 78, 80–81, 83–104, 106–114, 116–118, 121–123, 125, 128–130
asynchronous, 70, 77, 116
audio feedback, 112
authentic, 38, 83, 86–87, 89, 91, 95, 99, 106
autonomy, 30, 32

Bailey, 79
Baker, L., 87
Baker, S., 13
Bandura, 35
Bartolomeo-Maida, 85
Beattie, 41, 50
behavioral engagement, 1
belonging, 1, 9–12, 14, 23, 33, 48, 63, 70, 75–77
Berry, 21
Bombardieri, 47
Bostwick, 122

Bowen, 35, 41, 43
Brank, 72
Brookfield, 36
Brown, 86

Cameron, 87
Campus Compact, 102
career, 15–16, 24, 45, 50–55, 58, 65, 71, 78, 90–92, 128
Carver, 47
Case, 37, 70
Caspersz, 102
Cate, 105
Caulfield, 75
Cavanagh, 60, 63
Cell Press, 93
Center for Community College Student Engagement, 3, 47, 71
Chan, M., 1
Chan, S. C., 102
Chávez, 9, 10, 11, 20, 27
check-ins, 48, 70, 78, 110, 122
Cheng, 43
Chickering, 35, 107
Chiriac, 75
choice, 30–34, 38, 101, 114
cognitive engagement, 1
cohort, 17–18, 56, 71–72, 76, 90
Colbeck, 79
collaboration, 16, 27, 31, 39, 70–72, 74, 77, 84, 102
comfort zone, 14, 18, 31, 43, 80, 83, 93–95, 97–98, 106, 126
community college, 2, 10, 17, 36–37, 45, 47, 69, 71, 73, 121, 125
community-based learning, 79–80

computerized feedback, 129
confidence, 23, 33, 35, 43–45, 51,
    53–54, 83, 94–96, 98, 101–102,
    112, 115, 120–121, 125, 127–128
Connelly, 26
Cook, 84
Cooper, 36
counseling, 48, 50
creative thinking, 98–99
creativity, 38, 83, 98–101, 106
Crist, 47
Croes, 89
Crosby, 54
culture, 9, 11, 13, 49, 57, 78, 80,
    96–97, 101, 105
Cundell, 73
curriculum, 18–19, 27, 60, 62–63, 79,
    89–90, 102, 113, 125
Cuseo, 10

Daluba, 67
Davis, 36
Delfino, 1, 35
Demir, 35
demonstration, 59, 66–69, 81
depression, 49
Dickinson, 40
discussion, 16, 22, 38, 40, 60, 64,
    71–77, 80–81, 84, 91, 93–94, 125
diversity, 2, 30, 36–38, 96
Dixon, 16
Drago, 43
Ducasse, 123
Durham, 60, 71
Dweck, 122

Eccles, 25, 60
effort, 1, 2, 4, 10, 14, 18, 28, 33,
    35–37, 40, 42–43, 45–46, 57, 63,
    83, 91, 93, 107, 111, 120–122,
    125–126, 129
emotional engagement, 1
engaging outside of class, 38, 41, 43,
    57, 64, 66, 70–71, 83, 93

Ennen, 75
Espino-Bravo, 60
essay, 62–63, 98–99, 115, 123,
    126–127, 129
examples, 3, 4, 10–11, 15, 20–21, 24,
    27, 31, 36, 38, 40, 49, 54, 59–63,
    68, 70, 81, 86, 96, 121
exams, 28, 43, 52, 67–68, 86
expectations, 17, 27–30, 33, 54, 70,
    74–75, 106, 111, 118, 123, 126

face-to-face feedback, 70, 124
Facey, 118
family illness, 47
feedback, 3, 13, 18, 26, 32, 43, 49,
    57, 66–68, 71–73, 84, 107–125,
    127–130
Feldman, 129
Feltham, 120
Finney, 61
first day of class, 3, 9–16, 18, 20–28,
    30–33, 40, 64, 74, 99, 126,
first-generation, 41–42, 45, 47, 49, 56,
    60–61, 73, 76, 99, 100
Fleck, 102
focus groups, 71
formative assessment, 84, 108–111,
    113, 129
Forsythe, 120
foundational knowledge, 16, 26, 83,
    89, 95, 106
Friedman, 3

Garner, 119
Garrison, 69
Gehlbach, 13, 36
Goldberg, 72
Greenbank, 45, 50
Griffin, 59
group project, 75, 78, 81
Gubera, 59

Harber, 129
Harnish, 29

Harrington, 27, 32, 59, 73
Harris, 79
high-achieving students, 124–127, 130
Hollins, 2
Hrepic, 23
Hulleman, 65

icebreakers, 10, 12–18
illness, 47
interests, 10–12, 20, 30, 36–41, 45,
    50–52, 55, 61–63, 65, 75–76, 78,
    81, 99, 114
interviewing, 54, 95
introductions, 15, 19, 25, 32
Ismail, 87
Isnawati, 124

Johnson, 112
Joyce, 35
Jozwiak, 85

Karpova, 87
Kim, 67
Knowles, 3
Komarraju, 43
Kuh, 1, 2
Kurpis, 96

Landrum, 22
Lang, 10
large class, 11, 13–15, 41, 50, 60, 75
Latinx, 36, 43, 47, 49–50, 105
laws, 9
learning tasks, 20–21, 24, 27–28, 33,
    59–60, 66, 72, 83, 86, 90
lecture, 14, 20–21, 40, 59–62, 64–65,
    67–69, 76, 81, 84–85, 93, 111
Lei, 1, 14
Lightner, 28, 29
Linksz, 10
Lipnevich, 107, 113, 120, 125,
    129
Locke, 43, 93
loss, 47

Lowe, 120
Lucardie, 3, 18
Lundberg, 41

Malouff, 129
Manzano-Sancez, 43
marginalized groups, 2, 4, 97, 119–120
Marriott, 87
Martin, 16
Mather, 69
McClenney, 1, 2, 41, 50, 56, 107
McGinley, 9
McGuire, 53
mental health, 24, 47, 49
mentor(s), 15, 31, 39, 49–50, 53, 55,
    57, 70, 105
Micari, 46
Miller, A., 98
Miller, S., 69
Millis, 60
Milne, 66
Muddiman, 60, 62
Mushi, 60, 71, 107

names, 10–12, 15, 27, 32–33, 37, 76,
    129
National Center for Education
    Statistics, 2, 3
National Survey of Student
    Engagement, 3
network, 50, 53–54, 56, 58
Ngai, 105
Nicol, 107
Nilson, 11, 118
nontraditional age, 2–3, 47–48
Note–card activity, 63–65

office hours, 23, 43–44, 48–49,
    110–111
O'Neill, 108, 109
online course, 16, 32, 69, 74, 77–78,
    81, 116
online icebreaker, 16–17
online discussions, 63, 73–74, 81

oral feedback, 112–113
orientation, 1–2, 35, 119
outside of class, 38, 41, 43, 57, 64, 66, 70–71, 83, 93
Ozan, 86

Padron, 54
Parker, 85
part-time student, 2–3, 50, 56
passion, 18–19, 22, 29, 33, 52, 61–62, 65–66, 68, 101, 111, 128
Patchan, 108
Patel, 93
Payne, 79
Pecha Kucha, 37
peer conveyer-belt model, 118
peer feedback, 26, 71–73, 109, 115–118, 129
peer review, 18–19, 114–116, 118
peer support, 76
Peng, 88
Perna, 46
personal challenges, 46, 49
Phillips, 108
Pitt, 120
podcast, 23–24
portfolio, 98–99
precepting, 50–51
Prichard, 79
Priniski, 20, 62
professional network, 50, 53–54, 56, 58
professor–student relationship, 29, 35–42, 44, 46, 50, 52, 57, 120
projects, 12, 32, 60, 70–71, 75, 77–78, 80–81, 86, 89, 91–92, 103–105

quiz, 22, 42–43, 67, 84–85

Rabourn, 3
Rakow, 35
rapport, 3, 12, 19, 35
Rawle, 112

real–world experience, 25, 44, 60, 62, 83, 86–88, 90, 92, 94, 102
Redding, 35, 36
reflection, 18, 30–31, 38, 49, 64, 79, 97, 105, 123, 125
relationships, 3, 12, 35–41, 43, 46, 50, 52, 56–57, 73, 75–77, 95, 100, 120
research groups, 75
retention, 2, 36
revision, 109, 113, 119–121, 123, 125
Robinson, 20
Rodriguez, 62, 90, 107
Roehling, 71
Rogmans, 88
Rose, 69
rubrics, 111, 129

Sarfo, 79
Seider, 105
self–doubt, 43
self–efficacy, 25–26, 43, 83, 106, 120
sense of belonging, 1, 9–12, 14, 23, 33, 48, 63, 70, 75–77
service-learning, 102–103, 105–106
Sever, 69
Sheer, 40
Shin, 96
simulation, 87–89, 106
small groups, 9, 13, 39, 60, 63, 73, 75, 77, 80, 84, 109, 116
Smith, M., 115
Smith, T., 122
social media, 23–24, 87
Steingut, 27
Stern, 107
stories, 2–4, 10, 33, 49, 53, 59–61, 63, 80, 94–96, 118, 126
strengths, 22, 27, 31, 53, 98, 122, 127–128
summative assessments, 99, 109–111
Supiano, 36
surveys, 2–3, 13, 20–21, 25, 67, 122
Swanson, 71

Sweeney, 70, 71, 79
syllabus, 9, 15–16, 19–34, 74, 99, 126
synchronous meeting, 17–18, 69–70, 77, 81

Taras, 108
Taylor, 112
technical feedback, 107–108
Terrenzini, 83
Tews, 59, 66
textbook, 22, 61, 84
thought organizers, 73
transparency, 28, 90, 115
Tropman, 84
trust, 39, 49–53, 70, 75, 77

underrepresented groups, 2, 4, 13, 20, 34–35, 63, 119–120

ungraded assignments, 113

Van Hoye, 53
videos, 69–70, 78, 81, 87
Vilorio, 53
Voelkel, 112

Wang, 102
Wigfield, 25
Wilson, 35
Wlodkowski, 30, 107
Wollschleger, 83, 89
writing, 17, 19, 30–31, 38–39, 45, 53, 56–57, 62, 64, 85–87, 89, 94–95, 99–101, 104, 108–109, 115, 128
written feedback, 112–113, 121, 124
Wu, 2

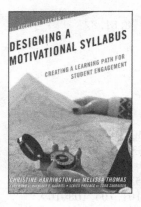